Introducing Functional Programming Using C#

Leveraging a New Perspective for OOP Developers

Vaskaran Sarcar

Apress®

Introducing Functional Programming Using C#: Leveraging a New Perspective for OOP Developers

Vaskaran Sarcar
Kolkata, West Bengal, India

ISBN-13 (pbk): 978-1-4842-9696-7   ISBN-13 (electronic): 978-1-4842-9697-4
https://doi.org/10.1007/978-1-4842-9697-4

Managing Director, Apress Media LLC: Welmoed Spahr
Acquisitions Editor: Smriti Srivastava
Development Editor: Laura Berendson
Editorial Project Manager: Mark Powers

Cover designed by eStudioCalamar

Cover image by BoliviaInteligente on Unsplash (www.unsplash.com)

Distributed to the book trade worldwide by Apress Media, LLC, 1 New York Plaza, New York, NY 10004, U.S.A. Phone 1-800-SPRINGER, fax (201) 348-4505, e-mail orders-ny@springer-sbm.com, or visit www. springeronline.com. Apress Media, LLC is a California LLC and the sole member (owner) is Springer Science + Business Media Finance Inc (SSBM Finance Inc). SSBM Finance Inc is a **Delaware** corporation.

For information on translations, please e-mail booktranslations@springernature.com; for reprint, paperback, or audio rights, please e-mail bookpermissions@springernature.com.

Apress titles may be purchased in bulk for academic, corporate, or promotional use. eBook versions and licenses are also available for most titles. For more information, reference our Print and eBook Bulk Sales web page at www.apress.com/bulk-sales.

Any source code or other supplementary material referenced by the author in this book is available to readers on GitHub (https://github.com/Apress). For more detailed information, please visit https://www.apress.com/gp/services/source-code.

Paper in this product is recyclable

This book is dedicated to all those developers who want to improve their applications and do not give up easily.

Table of Contents

About the Author

 **Vaskaran Sarcar** obtained his master's degree in software engineering from Jadavpur University, Kolkata (India), and his master's of computer application from Vidyasagar University, Midnapore (India). He was a National Gate Scholar (2007–2009) and has more than 12 years of experience in education and the IT industry. He devoted his early years (2005–2007) to the teaching profession at various engineering colleges, and later he joined HP India PPS R&D Hub in Bangalore. He worked at HP until August 2019. At the time of his retirement from HP, he was a senior software engineer and team lead. Vaskaran is following his passion and is now a full-time author. You can find him on LinkedIn at https://www.linkedin.com/in/vaskaransarcar and see all of his books at https://amazon.com/author/vaskaran_sarcar.

About the Technical Reviewers

Leandro Fernandes Vieira is a senior software engineer currently working for a leading payment solutions company. He earned his degree in system analysis and development from São Paulo State Technological College (FATEC-SP), Brazil. His realm of expertise includes the .NET stack and the C# and F# programming languages. He has a passion for programming and algorithms and likes to contribute to open-source projects; in fact, he is a creator of the RecordParser project, one of the fastest CSV parsers for .NET. He enjoys spending time with his family, walking in the park, hitting the gym, and listening to heavy-metal music.

You can reach him at `https://github.com/leandromoh/`.

Shekhar Kumar Maravi is a lead engineer in design and development, whose main interests are programming languages, algorithms, and data structures. He obtained his master's degree in computer science and engineering from the Indian Institute of Technology, Bombay (India). After graduation, he joined Hewlett-Packard's R&D Hub in India to work on printer firmware. Currently he is a technical lead engineer for automated pathology lab diagnostic devices in the Siemens Healthcare R&D division. He can be reached by email at `shekhar.maravi@gmail.com` or via LinkedIn at `https://www.linkedin.com/in/shekharmaravi`.

Acknowledgments

I thank the Almighty. I sincerely believe that only with His blessings could I complete this book. I also extend my deepest gratitude and thanks to the following people:

- **Leandro Fernandes Vieira and Paul Louth**: They allowed me to use the Curryfy library and language-ext library in this book. Leandro also joined the technical review team and provided many useful suggestions and improvements for this book.

- **Shekhar Kumar Maravi**: Shekhar was another technical reviewer for this book. He has been reviewing my books since 2015. Whenever I am in need, he provides me with support. Thank you one more time.

- **Smriti, Laura, and Mark**: Thanks to each of you for giving me another opportunity to work with you and Apress.

- **Shon, Kim, Nagarajan, and Vinoth**: Thanks to each of you for your exceptional support to improve my work.

Finally, I thank those people from the functional programming community who have shared their knowledge through online blogs, articles, courses, and books.

Introduction

Throughout the ages, prophets have suggested that most of us are not reaching our full potential. If you look at the great achievers in any field in the current world, you will find that they are hard workers, and they strive to keep improving. They put in extra effort to improve their skills, and in many cases, they even hire coaches to learn new techniques. Then, one day, they discover that all their hard work starts to pay off: they become masters in their chosen field.

The following quote from the Chinese philosopher Confucius perfectly summarizes this:

> *The will to win, the desire to succeed, the urge to reach your full potential...these are the keys that will unlock the door to personal excellence.*

Now let's apply this philosophy to programming. As a developer, are you reaching your full potential with C#? I may not know your reply, but I certainly know my answer. Even after working with C# for more than 14 years, there is still more to learn.

One evening I asked myself, how could I improve my C# skills? I could continue to try to learn new features and practice them, but intuitively, I knew there was an alternative answer. So, I started searching for tips and eventually discovered that most of the time I was using C# for object-oriented programming (OOP). Indeed, it is a perfect fit for OOP, and there is nothing wrong with this tendency. But what about functional programming (FP) using C#? It's not that I never used it (in fact, C# developers are very much familiar with LINQ), but I was not very conscious of it. So, I keep browsing through various resources, such as books, articles, and online courses. Eventually, I discovered that during its development, C# started embracing functional features too, and as a result, it has become a powerful hybrid language.

I became very interested in the topic and tried to learn more about it. From this time onward, I started facing challenges. There were some good resources, but I could not stitch them together to serve my needs. This is why I started documenting my notes when I was experimenting with using C# in a functional way. This book is a result of those efforts.

So, welcome to your journey through *Introducing Functional Programming Using C#: Leveraging a New Perspective for OOP Developers.*

C# is a powerful programming language, is well accepted in the programming world, and helps you make a wide range of applications. These are the primary reasons it is continuously growing in popularity and is always in high demand. So, it is not a surprise that existing and upcoming developers (for example, college students and programming lovers) are curious to learn C# and want to create their applications using it.

Many developers try to learn it in the shortest possible time frame and then claim they know C# well. In fact, many resources claim you can unlock the real power of C# in a day, a week, or a month. But is this true? I think not. Remember, I'm 14 years in and I'm still learning.

Malcolm Gladwell's 10,000-hour rule says that the key to achieving world-class expertise in any skill is, to a large extent, a matter of practicing the correct way, for a total of around 10,000 hours. So, even though we may claim that we know something very well, we actually know very little. Learning is a continuous process, with no end to it.

Then should we stop learning? Definitely, the answer is no. There is something called-effective learning. It teaches you how to learn fast to serve your need. This is the context where I like to remind you about the Pareto principle or 80-20 rule. This rule simply states that 80% of outcomes come from 20% of all causes. This is useful in programming too. When you truly learn the fundamental aspects of FP, you can use it effectively to improve your code. Most importantly, your confidence level will raise to a level from where you can learn more easily. This book is for those who acknowledge this fact. It helps you to understand the core principles of FP with plenty of Q&A sessions and exercises.

How Is This Book Organized?

The book has two major parts, which are as follows:

- Part I consists of the first three chapters, which start with an overview of functional programming (FP). Then we'll discuss functions and immutability in depth. These are the building blocks for FP and what you need to understand to move on to Part II of this book.

- C# is a multiparadigm language, and **Part II** reveals its potential. This part will cover how to harness the power of FP. In addition, two well-known external libraries, called Curryfy and language-ext, are discussed in this part. The first one is used in Chapter 5 when I discuss currying. The second one is used in Chapter 8 and Chapter 9 when I discuss functional error handling and the Monad pattern.

The best way to learn something is by analyzing case studies, asking questions about any doubts you have, and doing exercises. So, throughout this book, you will see interesting code snippets, "Q&A Sessions," and exercises. Each question in the "Q&A Sessions" sections is marked with <chapter_no>.<Question_no>. For example, 5.3 means question 3 from Chapter 5. You can use the simple exercises to evaluate your progress. Each question in these exercises is marked with E<chapter_no>.<Question_no>. For example, E6.2 means exercise 2 from Chapter 6.

The code examples and questions and answers (Q&As) are straightforward. I believe that by analyzing these Q&As and doing the exercises, you can verify your progress. They are presented to make your future learning easier and more enjoyable, but most importantly, they will help you become confident as a developer.

You can download all the source code of the book from the publisher's website, where you can also find an errata list for the book. I suggest that you visit that website to receive any important corrections or updates.

Prerequisite Knowledge

The target readers of this book are those who want to make the most of C# by harnessing the power of functional programming. I expect you to be familiar with .NET, C#, and OOP concepts. In fact, knowing about some advanced concepts such as delegates and lambda expressions can accelerate your learning. I assume that you know how to compile or run a C# application in Visual Studio. This book does not invest time in easily available topics, such as how to install Visual Studio on your system, how to write a "Hello World" program in C#, and so forth. Though I have used C# as the programming language, if you are familiar with a similar language like Java, you can apply that understanding to this book.

Who Is This Book For?

In short, read this book if you answer "yes" to the following questions:

- Are you familiar with .NET, C#, and basic object-oriented concepts such as polymorphism, inheritance, abstraction, and encapsulation?

- Are you familiar with some of the advanced concepts in C# such as delegates, lambda expressions, and generics?

- Do you know how to set up your coding environment?

- Do you want to develop your functional programming skills?

- Are you interested in knowing how the core constructs of C# can help you in FP?

You probably shouldn't pick this book if the answer is "yes" to any of the following questions:

- Are you looking for a C# tutorial or reference book?

- Are you not ready to experiment with FP with a programming language that was primarily developed for OOP?

- Do you despise Windows, Visual Studio, or .NET?

Useful Software

These are the important tools that I use in this book:

- While writing this book, I had the latest edition of Visual Studio Community 2022 (64-bit, version 17.5.4). All the programs were tested with C# 11 and .NET 7.

- Nowadays the C# language version is automatically selected based on your project's target framework(s) so that you can always get the highest compatible version by default. In the latest versions, Visual Studio doesn't allow the UI to change the value, but you can change it by editing the `.csproj` file.

- As per a new rule, C# 11 is supported only on .NET 7 and newer versions. C# 10 is supported only on .NET 6 and newer versions. C# 9 is supported only on .NET 5 and newer versions. C# 8.0 is supported only on .NET Core 3.x and newer versions. If you are interested in the C# language versioning, you can visit `https://docs.microsoft.com/en-us/dotnet/csharp/language-reference/configure-language-version`.

- The community edition is free of cost. If you do not use the Windows operating system, you can still use the free Visual Studio Code, which is a source-code editor developed by Microsoft to support Windows, Linux, or Mac operating systems. At the time of this writing, Visual Studio 2022 for Mac is also available, but I did not test my code on it.

Guidelines for Using This Book

Here are some suggestions so you can use the book more effectively:

- This book suits you best if you are familiar with some advanced features in C# such as delegates and lambda expressions. If not, please read about these topics before you start reading this book.

- I organized the chapters in an order that can help grow your functional thinking with each chapter. Therefore, I recommend reading the chapters sequentially.

- The code in this book should give you the expected output in future versions of C#/Visual Studio as well. Though I believe that the results should not vary in other environments, you know the nature of software: it is naughty. So, I recommend that if you want to see the exact same output as in the book, you mimic the same environment.

- You can download and install the Visual Studio IDE from `https://visualstudio.microsoft.com/downloads/` (see Figure I-1).

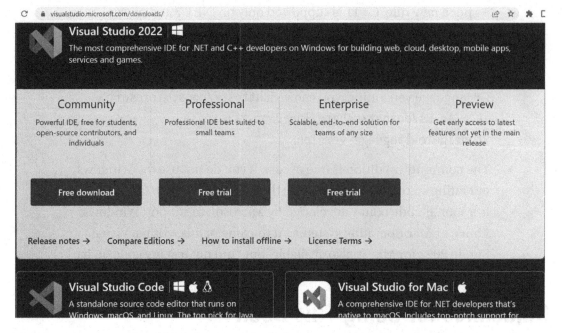

Figure I-1. *Download link for Visual Studio 2022, Visual Studio for Mac, and Visual Studio Code*

Note At the time of this writing, this link works fine and the information is correct. But the link and policies may change in the future. The same comment applies to all the links mentioned in this book.

Source Code

All the source code used in this book can be found at https://github.com/apress/introduction-functional-programming-cs.

Conventions Used in This Book

In many places, I point you to Microsoft's documentation. Why? As the creator of C#, Microsoft is the primary authority on each feature.

I've used top-level statements heavily in this book. Consequently, there is no need for me to explicitly write the Main method for console applications. You understand that using this technique, I minimized the code lengths. When you use top-level statements, the C# compiler does the necessary job on your behalf in the background. Top-level statements have been supported since C# 9.0.

I also like to add that I enabled `implicit usings` for my C# projects. The `implicit usings` feature automatically adds common `global using` directives for the type of project you are building. Starting from C#10.0, this feature is also supported. Otherwise, I had to add the necessary directives to my programs manually.

Finally, all the output/code in the book uses the same font and structure. To draw your attention in some places, I have used bold fonts. For example, consider the following output fragment (taken from Chapter 3 where I discuss external immutability):

```
Understanding Mutability and Immutability.
Name: Sam, ID:1
The emp1's hashcode:43942917
The temp's hashcode:43942917
Name: Sam, ID:2
The emp1's hashcode:59941933
The temp's hashcode:43942917
```

Final Words

Congratulations, you have chosen a programming language to experiment with a paradigm that will assist you throughout your career. As you learn and review these concepts, I suggest you write your code instead of copying and pasting it; there is no better way to learn.

Upon completing this book, you'll be confident about FP and the value it provides you.

PART I

Getting Familiar with Functional Programming

Part I consists of three chapters. It starts with an overview of functional programming (FP). Then it discusses functions and immutability in depth. Specifically, Part I covers the following topics:

- **Chapter 1** provides a quick overview of functional programming and describes the important characteristics of FP. This chapter compares FP and object-oriented programming (OOP) and also points out the key benefits of using FP.

- Functions are the building blocks for FP. **Chapter 2** provides a detailed discussion of functions and covers first-order and higher-order functions. This chapter also shows a simple technique for refactoring impure functions into pure functions and making your code more "functional."

- Immutability is another important characteristic of FP. **Chapter 3** discusses this topic in depth with examples of external, internal, shallow, and popsicle immutability using features available in C#.

In brief, these are the building blocks for FP and the foundations you'll need to understand before reading Part II of this book.

CHAPTER 1

Functional Programming Overview

You can reach a destination using different vehicles. If the destination is well connected to transportation routes, you can use a car, a bus, a train, or an airplane. If the destination is nearby, you may opt for a bicycle. If you are health conscious, you may prefer to walk. This is simple to understand. Now think about some special scenarios: you need to reach your destination as soon as possible, but it is not a nearby location. Are you going to walk? The answer is no. In a situation like this, you will want to use a vehicle to reach your destination faster. But when you are not in a hurry or want to avoid a crowded bus, you may prefer to walk. Depending on the context, one approach might be a better fit compared to others.

The programming world is no different. You can use different programming styles to create the same application. Each approach has its pros and cons. Based on the given constraints in an application, you might prefer one approach over another. If you are aware of multiple routes, you can choose the approach that suits your needs best.

C# Supports Multiple Paradigms

Different programming languages usually target different coding styles/paradigms. But when programming language developers introduce new features to make a language richer, the features may not follow the original programming style; instead, languages can support multiple programming paradigms. As a result, over time these computer languages become hybrid in nature. The associated benefit is obvious: you can make an application by choosing the approach that suits your needs best (or even mixing the approaches). For example, an object-oriented programming (OOP) developer may use the functional style of coding in some code segments to reap some particular benefit.

© Vaskaran Sarcar 2023
V. Sarcar, *Introducing Functional Programming Using C#*, https://doi.org/10.1007/978-1-4842-9697-4_1

C# and F# are .NET programming languages. F# is primarily a functional language, but it supports the .NET object model. On the other hand, C# is primarily object-oriented, but it supports several functional features. Particularly, in the latest versions, you'll see plenty of support for functional programming. Let's see what Microsoft says about this (see https://learn.microsoft.com/en-us/dotnet/standard/linq/concepts-terminology-functional-transformation):

> *Historically, general-purpose functional programming languages, such as ML, Scheme, Haskell, and F#, have been primarily of interest to the academic community. Although it has always been possible to write pure functional transformations in C# and Visual Basic, the difficulty of doing so has not made it an attractive option to most programmers. In recent versions of these languages, however, new language constructs such as lambda expressions and type inference make functional programming much easier and more productive.*

So, using C#, you can also combine different styles of coding in an application. Most importantly, to implement the key ideas in functional programming (FP), you can use C# instead of learning a new programming language. Throughout the book, we'll look into these possibilities.

Functions and Methods Are Equivalent in C#

Like any other OOP developer, you may like using the term *method* instead of *function*. In C#, you typically place methods inside a class because they do not exist independently. Since C# primarily supports OOP, you see this kind of design often.

It should not be a surprise to you that functions are the building blocks for FP. The online link https://learn.microsoft.com/en-us/dotnet/standard/linq/refactor-pure-functions says the following:

> *However, in C#, functions are called methods.*

Now it is clear that conceptually a method and a function are the same. You see this terminology difference because these two different paradigms treat functions differently. In this book, we are exploring functional programming. So, I'll be using the term *function* instead of *method* in the corresponding places.

In Chapter 2, you'll see that in addition to the traditional methods, there are other ways to represent functions.

Q&A Session

1.1 C# primarily follows OOP, but you are using it in the functional style. This helps us avoid learning a new programming language, but are you saying that learning an FP-based computer language is a bad idea?

Not at all. Developing your knowledge and learning a new programming language are always good ideas. If you know functional languages like F# or Haskell, no one is restricting you from using them. But in a real-world project, you may not have that freedom. For example, if you are working on a project that uses only C#, you have only one option: coding with C#. But C# is a multiparadigm language, and it supports functional programming. This means that by using some of its features, you can bring the power of functional programming to an existing project.

Second, you may not have the time or motivation to learn a new programming language to fulfill some specific needs in a project. In such cases, it is always helpful to implement the concept using known features.

Finally, many existing features in C# have been developed following the functional style of coding. Instead of blindly using them, if you understand the context, you can enjoy your learning.

Important Characteristics of FP

Though FP is a programming paradigm, it does not specify how the concepts should be implemented in a programming language. As a result, a programming language that follows FP can support many different features to implement these concepts. At a high level, FP has the following characteristics:

- It treats functions as first-class citizens.

- It prefers immutability.

- It prefers pure functions.

- It follows declarative programming.

Let's take a quick look at these bullet points. You can surely guess that we'll cover all these points in more detail in the upcoming chapters.

FP Treats Functions as First-Class Citizens

FP treats functions as first-class citizens. What does this mean? This means you can use them like any other type. For example, you can assign a function to a variable, pass it as an argument to another function, or use it as a return type. It is possible to store them in data structures too. When someone says that a programming language supports first-class functions, you can assume that the programming language supports these concepts. So, you can think of first-class functions as a programming language feature.

Since we are trying to adopt functional programming, the following questions may come to your mind:

- What is a function type in C#?

- Does C# have first-class functions?

In C#, delegate types can represent functions. If you are familiar with Func (or Action) delegates or if you are a lambda lover, probably you know this answer, and you are already familiar with the usage.

To clarify, let's consider the Func<int,int> type. You know that this is a delegate type and it encapsulates a function that accepts one int parameter and returns a value of type int. Let's consider a sample line of code that is as follows:

```
Func<int, int> doubleMaker = x => x * 2;
```

This code says the following:

- I have a function that takes an integer, multiplies it with 2, and returns the result.

- I have assigned this function to the variable doubleMaker.

Since the function is assigned to the variable doubleMaker, a developer can write something like int result = doubleMaker(5);.

You can also pass this function to another function. Demonstration 1 shows such a usage.

Demonstration 1

In the following program, doubleMaker is an instance of Func<int, int>, and it is used as a variable. I pass this variable to another function, called GetResult.

Note   I remind you that I have heavily used top-level statements and enabled `implicit usings` for the C# projects in this book. These features came in C# 9.0 and C#10.0 respectively.

```csharp
using static System.Console;

int temp = 5;
Func<int, int> doubleMaker = x => x * 2;
int result = Container.GetResult(doubleMaker,temp);
WriteLine(result);

static class Container
{
    public static int GetResult(Func<int,int> f, int x)
    {
        return f(x);
    }
}
```

Output

The output is easy to predict. Since I have passed the integer 5 as an input (along with the function variable `doubleMaker`), the program outputs 10.

Analysis

Let's analyze the key steps in this program. First I declare a function using a delegate and name the function variable `doubleMaker`. I then pass this variable to invoke the `GetResult` function. So, the following points are clear:

- You can assign a function to a variable.

- You can pass a function as an argument to another function.

As you progress more with learning FP, it will be natural for you to use functions as return types or store them in a data structure. So, we can conclude that C# indeed supports first-class functions.

FP Prefers Immutability

Immutability is a design choice, and it is one of the fundamental principles of FP. In this context, I'd like to quote Microsoft again. The online link https://learn.microsoft.com/en-us/archive/msdn-magazine/2010/april/fsharp-basics-an-introduction-to-functional-programming-for-net-developers says the following:

> *Imperative programming emphasizes the use of mutable variables whereas functional programming uses immutable values.*

Chapter 3 of this book discusses many aspects of immutability. In the .NET world, it means that once you initialize (or create) a type, you should not change its internal state at a later stage. Immutability is a big topic. For now, let's have a quick review.

Author's note   In Chapter 3, you'll see different variations of immutability. But in every case, the core idea is the same: once you make a type that does not allow continuous changes to its state (or the state of its instances), it is considered immutable in some sense.

Demonstration 2

Suppose I have a program that starts with a list of names. Later, I clear the content of this list and add new names. The following program demonstrates this:

```
using static System.Console;

List<string> names = new() { "Sam", "Bob" };
WriteLine("The list includes the following names:");
names.ForEach(x=> WriteLine(x));

// Removing existing names
names.Clear();
// Adding two new names
names.Add("Kate");
names.Add("Jack");

WriteLine("\nThe list includes the following names:");
names.ForEach(x => WriteLine(x));
```

> **Note** Removing the lambda expression, you can simply the line `names.ForEach(x => WriteLine(x));` as `names.ForEach(WriteLine);`.

Output

Let's verify the output.

```
The list includes the following names:
Sam
Bob

The list includes the following names:
Kate
Jack
```

You can see that the list contained two names, `Sam` and `Bob`, in the beginning. Later I cleared the content of this list and added two new names. This kind of update is called a *destructive update* because you have lost the original content. The situation can be worse if you encounter runtime exceptions. **FP does not like this. It prefers immutability**. The key idea is that once created, variables should not be reassigned or modified.

Now think for a moment: if you work on immutable variables, you know that once initialized, these variables cannot change their values. So, the term *variable* does not make sense in those contexts. **This is the reason you will hear the term *value* instead of *variable* in functional programming.**

Q&A Session

1.2 How does immutability fit into functional programming?

Immutability prevents nasty bugs from implicit dependencies, destructive updates, and state mutations. These are aligned with FP's goal. Immutable types are thread-safe; therefore, in a multithreaded environment, they make your programming life easy. Shortly, you'll learn about pure functions and side effects. Then you'll understand that these immutable types can help you avoid side effects too. In Chapter 6, you'll see that immutable types are also useful to avoid temporal coupling. There are many more benefits; once you finish this book, you'll be able to find those benefits in other areas as well.

1.3 While discussing destructive updates, you said that the situation becomes worse if you encounter runtime exceptions. Can you give an example to demonstrate such a situation?

Consider Demonstration 3.

Demonstration 3

To answer the previous question (1.3), I'm going to modify Demonstration 2. Let's assume that the program needs to display the names along with the number of characters that are present in the name. The following is a typical implementation that contains a possible bug. Why is there a possible bug? I start with a list of names called names, and then I use the following code segment in this program:

```
int random = new Random().Next(0, 2);
string? newName = random > 0 ? "Jack": null;
// Adding a new name
names.Add(newName);
```

You can see that before I add a name to the list, I generate a random number. If the number is greater than 0, I'll add this name; otherwise, I'll add a null. (Yeah, I know, it is bad! But I want to produce the bug easily.)

Here is the complete program (notice the important changes in bold):

```
using static System.Console;

WriteLine("Analyzing destructive updates.");

List<string> names = new() { "Sam", "Bob" };
WriteLine("The list includes the following:");
names.ForEach(x => WriteLine($"Name: {x},length:{x.Length}"));

int random = new Random().Next(0, 2);
string? newName = random > 0 ? "Jack": null;
// Adding a new name
names.Add(newName);
WriteLine("\nThe list includes the following names:");
names.ForEach(x => WriteLine($"Name: {x},length:{x.Length}"));
```

Output

Here is some sample output when everything goes well and it was able to add a new name successfully:

```
Analyzing destructive updates.
The list includes the following:
Name: Sam,length:3
Name: Kate,length:4

The list includes the following names:
Name: Sam,length:3
Name: Kate,length:4
Name: Jack,length:4
```

But based on the generated random number (when it is 0), this program can throw the following runtime exception:

```
System.NullReferenceException: 'Object reference not set to an instance of
an object.'
x was null.
```

Analysis

This program shows that a destructive update can raise a runtime error. As developers, we do not like to see a program crash at runtime. FP's philosophy is simple: avoid destructive updates. When I discuss immutability in depth in Chapter 3, you'll see that we can avoid this kind of update in our program.

FP Prefers Pure Functions

FP wants you to use pure functions as much as possible. Microsoft (see `https://learn.microsoft.com/en-us/dotnet/standard/linq/refactor-pure-functions`) echoes this by saying the following:

> *The common nomenclature in functional programming is that you refactor programs using pure functions.*

Which functions are pure? The previous link states that **a function is pure if it satisfies the following characteristics:**

- It's consistent. Given the same set of input data, it will always return the same output value.

- It has no side effects. The function does not change any variables or data of any type outside of the function.

The function that does not satisfy any of these conditions is called an **impure function**.

Demonstration 4

You will learn more about purity and side effects shortly. For now, it will be sufficient if you understand the following program:

```
using static System.Console;

WriteLine(AddFiveTo(2));
WriteLine(GetRandomNumber(2));

static int AddFiveTo(int input)
{
    return input + 5;
}
static int GetRandomNumber(int input)
{
    Random random = new();
    return random.Next(input, input + 5);
}
```

Output

Here are some probable outputs from this program:

Sample Output-1:

```
7
3
```

Sample Output-2:

7

6

Sample Output-3:

7

4

And so on. You can see that given input 2, GetRandomNumber returns different values. Since the result is inconsistent, you can conclude that this is an impure function.

Now, look into the AddFive function. You can see that AddFiveTo is consistent; it always returns 7 if the input is 2. You can also see that this function depends on the supplied input only; it does not change any variables or data of any type outside of the function. So, this function does not have any side effect. Since both conditions for purity are satisfied, we can conclude that AddFiveTo is a pure function.

Discussion of Side Effects

Let's discuss side effects. Look at the following possibilities:

- *Case 1*: Your function keeps modifying a static variable.

- *Case 2*: You modify the function argument by passing a parameter as a reference.

- *Case 3*: Your function raises an exception for certain cases.

- *Case 4*: Your function accepts user input and prints some message in a console window.

The first two cases are easy to understand: they cause side effects. Why? In each case, you mutate the values. As a result, given the same input, the same function produces different outputs. You may still wonder about case 3 and case 4. Let's take a look at them.

To demonstrate case 3, I've written the following function inside the Sample class. Obviously, it is bad.

```
class Sample
{
    public static int GetResult(int a)
    {
```

```
        int random = new Random().Next(0,2);
        return a / random;
    }
}
```

The first problem is obvious: you cannot predict the result in advance. For example, the following line:

```
int result = Sample.GetResult(6);
```

can give you valid data, or it can raise the following exception (when the divisor random becomes 0): System.DivideByZeroException: 'Attempted to divide by zero.'

Throwing an exception always forces you to think about gracefully handling the exception; otherwise, your program crashes, which is an example of the worst possible side effect. In fact, exceptions indicate indeterminism in the code.

I discuss case 4 in the section "Functions with I/O," which is coming next.

Functions with I/O

It should not be a surprise that a meaningful program often needs to accept user input and display the output. So, you may be wondering, if a function displays the output of a program, is it a side effect? Let's analyze this. If a function asks a user to pass a URL to display a webpage, the result can vary when the internet connection becomes unstable or the server is down. As a result, the same function can potentially produce different results. In fact, thinking about the output can make you even more uncomfortable. Consider the case when a function queries a user by outputting text to the console something like the following:

```
Console.WriteLine("Enter a number:");
```

Did you notice that the state of the system has changed, and returning the system to its previous state is impossible now? You can see that when a function needs to depend on the external world, there is no escape. You may argue that this is an intended scenario, but following the FP paradigm, it is still considered a side effect. In fact, a purely mathematical function often needs to communicate the result using the I/O. So, some of your code segments will have to be impure.

Now the next question is, which part of the code segments can be impure? A common guideline for this type of situation is that you should try to separate the functions that perform the I/O from the functions that perform the actual computation. The functions that perform those computations should be the pure function in the functional world. In C#, we can mix them, but to follow a functional style of coding, keep this suggestion in your mind.

In this book, I often compare OOP-style coding with an equivalent functional style of coding with complete programs. When I refactor the imperative code to functional code, I focus on the key aspects. Normally, I do not change the Main method (aka function) that handles the I/O operations. Remember, since I use top-level statements to demonstrate programs, you will not explicitly see the presence of the Main method. For example, in .NET 7, I can run a program that consists of a single line as follows:

```
Console.WriteLine("Hello, reader!");
```

This is a big simplification compared to older versions of C#, where you need to explicitly define the Main method and use the "using statements" at the beginning of your file.

Author's note If needed, you can learn about top-level statements at https://learn. microsoft.com/en-us/dotnet/csharp/whats-new/tutorials/top-level-statements.

POINT TO NOTE

In the OOP style, it is a common practice to encapsulate data and methods inside a class. But in the functional style of coding, it is common to separate the functions from the data. The discussion of side effects should give you the idea that FP encourages us to work on pure functions and minimize the side effects.

Are Side Effects Bad?

Up until now we have been discussing function purity following the formal definition. Now the question is, are impure functions acceptable? Here are my thoughts on them:

- We make assumptions about purity to some extent. This is because any function can fail because of some factors that are beyond our control. Consider the case of the "out of memory" error when your code did not cause the error, but it came from someone else's code, which was executing in a parallel environment. Or, consider the case when the operating system (OS) itself crashes. If you consider cases like this, no function is 100 percent pure, and this is the sad truth! So, when we talk about side effects, we ignore the factors that are beyond our control.

- Impurity does not always indicate something bad. Also, side effects are often desirable in certain places. To illustrate this, let's consider the example of a database update or consider the case where you work with a function that logs data including the current date and time. What do you think about these operations? You understand that to bring the theoretical "concept of purity," you cannot introduce unwanted complexities and compromise the overall performance of your program.

The key idea is that you should avoid side effects as much as possible to make your code more maintainable. For example, you can isolate the I/O operations from the actual computations. (You will learn more about this in Chapter 6 when I discuss the Functional Core, Imperative Shell pattern.) Keeping a similar goal in mind, when you refactor a code where the user interface (UI) layer talks to the business logic layer, you first attempt to minimize the side effects in the business logic layer.

POINT TO REMEMBER

In the context of purity and side effects, you can remember the following points:

- Any side effect indicates a visible "state change" of a program.

- A pure function is "pure" to some extent. We cannot avoid all possible circumstances. For example, during an execution of a C# function, an exception can be thrown because of various factors. Typical examples include insufficient memory or any other operating system errors.

- This means we cannot control every possible side effect. In general, you should focus on those parts that you can control.

- Finally, you should not conclude that an impure function is a bad thing. In OOP, you probably have seen that we want dynamic behavior in many applications, and that behavior is very much desirable there. In fact, a normal program that tries to update a database has a "desirable" side effect. Here we are studying pure functions following the formal definitions, and this is the reason we are focusing on purity. As you progress on this topic, these topics will be clearer to you.

Q&A Session

1.4 Why does FP like pure functions?

There are many reasons behind this. Let me show you some of those benefits:

- Since these functions result in the same output, you can write test cases against a consistent or reliable output.

- This consistent nature can provide you with huge benefits when you focus on parallelization.

In fact, once you get the result from an execution of a pure function, you can avoid the further execution of this function. This is because, once computed, this computed value will not change anymore.

1.5 Why do FP developers try to avoid side effects?

Side effects can change program states. This characteristic can compromise the correctness of the code. In addition, a method that has side effects does not depend entirely on program inputs. Because of this, it is difficult to predict the program's behavior in advance. So, these side effects compromise the understandability of the code too. In addition, if you work in a multithreaded environment and have methods that cause side effects, you need to worry about thread synchronizations. It is because you know that mutable variables lead to implicit dependencies and can cause a lot of nasty bugs, particularly in a concurrent program.

FP Follows a Declarative Style

Functional programming follows the declarative style of coding. What does this mean? A declarative style focuses on "**What** do we want?" instead of saying something like "Do this step, then do that step to get the result." When you mention a step-by-step approach to solving a problem, the approach is imperative, not declarative. So, the imperative style of programming describes how to solve the problem. The following statements will make the concept clearer to you:

- **Imperative programming approach**: Traverse the employee list sequentially. If the employee's age is 30 or more, show the employee's detail.

- **Declarative (functional) programming approach**: From a given list, display the details of the employees who are 30 years or older.

Demonstration 5

I will now show you a sample program that follows an imperative style of coding. OOP developers are quite familiar with this style. Given a list of numbers, the following program picks the numbers that are greater than 30 (notice the important segment in bold):

```
using static System.Console;

WriteLine("Using an imperative style of coding.");
List<int> numbers = new() { 10, 20, 30, 40, 50 };
// Imperative style
WriteLine("The list includes the following:");
foreach (int number in numbers)
{
    Write(number + "\t");
}
```

```
WriteLine("\nAges that are more than 30:");
foreach (int number in numbers)
{
    if (number > 30)
    {
        Write(number + "\t");
    }
}
```

Output

This program produces the following output:

```
Using an imperative style of coding.
The list includes the following:
10      20      30      40      50
Ages that are more than 30:
40      50
```

Now let's see how a functional programmer can write an equivalent program. Functional programmers like to use expressions, not statements. Why? This choice makes the code more declarative. Probably you know that System.Linq in C# is functional in nature. So, a functional programmer may like to use the built-in support and refactor the previous program; this is shown in the following demonstration.

Demonstration 6

Here is the refactored program (notice the important changes in bold):

```
using static System.Console;

WriteLine("Using the declarative style of coding.");
List<int> numbers = new() { 10, 20, 30, 40, 50 };
WriteLine("The list includes the following:");
numbers.ForEach(x => Write(x + "\t"));
WriteLine("\nAges that are more than 30:");
```

```
numbers.Where(x => x > 30)
    .Select(x => x)
    .ToList()
    .ForEach(x => Write(x + "\t"));
```

Output

It should be no surprise that you see an equivalent output (that you saw in Demonstration 5):

```
Using the declarative style of coding.
The list includes the following:
10      20      30      40      50
Ages that are more than 30:
40      50
```

Q&A Session

1.6 You said that FP developers prefer the declarative style of coding. Do you think that the declarative style is better than the imperative style?

No. Each approach has its pros and cons. Remember that our goal is to take the best from each approach.

Let's see the advantages of the declarative style of coding. The imperative style instructs how to perform the computation, so the order of execution of the statements is important. But the declarative style focuses on what to be computed, not on "how it's to be computed." **So, it helps you vary the function invocation calls**. For example, given the list shown in the previous demo, each of the following code segments (segment-1 and segment-2) will produce the identical result (notice that I have altered the function calls in the top two lines in these segments):

```
// Segment-1
numbers.Where(x => x > 30)
        .Select(x => x)
        .ToList()
        .ForEach(x => Write(x + "\t"));
```

```
// Segment-2
numbers.Select(x => x)
       .Where(x => x > 30)
       .ToList()
       .ForEach(x => Write(x + "\t"));
```

1.7 I am not very familiar with LINQ. Can you compare imperative versus declarative programming with another example?

I suggest you learn and test some basic operations using LINQ. These will help you understand this book and functional programming better. If you are not familiar with LINQ, let me show you another example.

I assume every OOP developer is familiar with `if-else` constructs. Consider the following code where the program starts with an integer (`flag`) that has the initial value 0. Then I generate two random numbers, `random1` and `random2`, and display them. So, you'll see the following code:

```
int flag = 0;
int random1 = new Random().Next(0,2);
int random2 = new Random().Next(10,15);
WriteLine($"The random number 1 is: {random1}");
WriteLine($"The random number 2 is: {random2}");
```

Later I'll evaluate two `if` conditions. If `random1` is an even number, I'll increment the `flag` value by 1. Then I'll check whether `random2` is greater than or equal to 13. If this condition is satisfied, I'll increment the flag value by 2. Here is the code:

```
if (random1 % 2 == 0)
{
    flag++;
}

if (random2 >= 13)
{
    flag+=2;
}
WriteLine($"The flag is:{flag}");
```

21

Now let me write an equivalent code using expressions. This time I use the ternary conditional operator (I renamed flag to flag1 and kept both program segments in the same file for your comparison purposes):

```
int flag1 = 0;
flag1+=(random1 % 2 == 0 ? 1 : 0)
      + (random2 >= 13 ? 2 : 0);
WriteLine($"The flag1 is:{flag1}");
```

You can see that two if blocks are replaced with two lines of code now (for better readability I made two lines; otherwise, they could be accommodated in a single line too). This example shows that declarative code can help you write concise code.

Demonstration 7

Here is the complete program that shows the usage of all the parts that I discussed:

```
using static System.Console;
#region imperative
int flag = 0;
int random1 = new Random().Next(0, 2);
int random2 = new Random().Next(10, 15);
WriteLine($"The random number 1 is: {random1}");
WriteLine($"The random number 2 is: {random2}");
if (random1 % 2 == 0)
{
    flag++;
}

if (random2 >= 13)
{
    flag += 2;
}
WriteLine($"The flag is: {flag}");
#endregion

#region declarative
int flag1 = 0;
```

```
flag1 += (random1 % 2 == 0 ? 1 : 0)
      + (random2 >= 13 ? 2 : 0);
WriteLine($"The flag1 is: {flag1}");
#endregion
```

Output

Here are some sample outputs to demonstrate that both approaches produce the equivalent output (notice that flag values range from 0 to 3):

Sample output-1:

```
The random number 1 is: 1
The random number 2 is: 14
The flag is: 2
The flag1 is: 2
```

Sample output-2:

```
The random number 1 is: 0
The random number 2 is: 11
The flag is: 1
The flag1 is: 1
```

Sample output-3:

```
The random number 1 is: 1
The random number 2 is: 12
The flag is: 0
The flag1 is: 0
```

Sample output-4:

```
The random number 1 is: 0
The random number 2 is: 13
The flag is: 3
The flag1 is: 3
```

FP vs. OOP

Each coding style has associated pros and cons. This book uses C# as the programming language, which primarily supports OOP. But as mentioned, C# also supports FP. So, you may like to know some of the differences between these approaches. Once you learn about FP principles, you'll understand that these principles are orthogonal to each other. Microsoft (`https://learn.microsoft.com/en-us/dotnet/standard/linq/functional-vs-imperative-programming`) says the following:

> *Functional programming is a form of declarative programming. In contrast, most mainstream languages, including object-oriented programming (OOP) languages such as C#, Visual Basic, C++, and Java, were designed to primarily support imperative (procedural) programming.*

From this quote, you can understand that OOP developers primarily follow the imperative style of coding to make their applications. You will also notice that to emphasize declarative coding that FP lovers like to use a single expression (remember the use of LINQ?) instead of using a series of statements. Since we already covered imperative versus declarative style in the previous section, I won't elaborate on this again.

POINT TO REMEMBER

OOP follows the imperative style of coding where you instruct the computer by saying something like "Do this and then do that." This style of coding is also termed *algorithmic programming*. But FP follows the declarative style.

The second most important thing is that tracking the state changes plays a vital role in the imperative approach, but it is nonexistent in the functional approach.

Finally, the classes or structures are the basic building blocks in the imperative style of coding, whereas functions are treated as first-class citizens and are important in the functional approach.

I'll finish this discussion with Michael Feather's quote (see `https://twitter.com/mfeathers/status/29581296216?lang=en`), shown here:

> *OO makes code understandable by encapsulating moving parts. FP makes code understandable by minimizing moving parts.*

FP Benefits

FP offers some important benefits to programmers. The following points include some of them:

- FP promotes shorter and cleaner code. Often these are very readable.

- FP likes pure functions. You can manage and test them easily.

- In a multithread environment, you can write better code that can prevent traditional problems such as lost updates and deadlocks. Let me remind you about a typical scenario: in a multithreaded application, avoiding race conditions is a big concern for us. Often, you introduce locks to avoid them. But these locks are expensive. Now the question is, how can you avoid them? One probable solution is to follow the functional style of coding in certain code segments. Since FP uses immutable types, you can write lock-free code.

- FP helps you write independent code segments. These are essential when you want to introduce parallelism.

- Finally, FP shows you a new perspective on development. If you are aware of other paradigms such as OOP, you can combine them with FP to make better applications.

Q&A Session

1.8 At the beginning of the chapter, you told me that I can follow different programming styles to create an application. Can you let me know about some of the well-known programming styles?

At a high level, you can consider imperative and declarative as the two major types of programming. With further research, you'll see that OOP, procedural programming, etc., follows the imperative style of coding. Functional programming (FP), logic programming, etc., follows the declarative style. The wiki at `https://en.wikipedia.org/wiki/Programming_paradigm` discusses programming paradigms with supportive materials. If interested, you can take a look.

Exercises

E1.1 Can you give examples of some built-in pure functions in C#?

E1.2 Suppose there is a function that demands you pass a file path to show you the content of the file. Will you consider it a pure function?

E1.3 What do you do when you cannot avoid using an impure function?

E1.4 C# supports first-class functions. What does this mean?

E1.5 This chapter shows that you can assign a function to a variable or pass it as an argument to another function. Can you write a program where you use a function as a return type?

E1.6 "A pure function can depend on an impure function." Is this true?

E1.7 "An impure function can call a pure function." Is this true?

E1.8 In the following code segment, can you point out the pure and impure functions?

```
class Sample
{
    public static bool OpsDone{get;set;}
    public static void ChangeStatus()
    {
        OpsDone = !OpsDone;
    }
    public static int FindDifference(int a, int b)
    {
        return Math.Abs(a - b);
    }
    public static int GetSquare(int x)
    {
        return x * x;
    }
    public static int GetCube(int x)
    {
        OpsDone = true;
        return x * x * x;
    }
```

```csharp
    public int Divide(int a, int b)
    {
        return a / b;
    }

    internal double DividePositiveNumbers(PositiveNumber a,
      PositiveNumber b)
    {
        return a.Number / b.Number;
    }

    public void DoSomething(string input)
    {
        WriteLine($"Doing some specific operation based on
         {input}.");
        OpsDone = true;
    }

    public static int Get75()
    {
        return 75;
    }

    public DateTime GetCurrentTime()
    {
        return DateTime.Now;
    }
}

class PositiveNumber
{
    public double Number { get; }

    public PositiveNumber(int input)
    {
        Number = input > 0 ? input : 1;
    }
}
```

Summary

This chapter gave you an overview of functional programming. It answered the following questions:

- What is a functional style of coding?

- How does FP differ from OOP?

- What are the characteristics of FP?

- How can built-in C# constructs help you in FP?

- What are the benefits of FP?

Solutions to Exercises

Here are the solutions. You know that there are multiple ways to solve a problem. So, if you implement a different solution than the one provided but fulfill the criteria of the given problem, it is OK. The same comment applies to all solution sets in this book.

E1.1

The System.Math class has many such functions such as Abs, Ceiling, or Floor. You know that the output of Math.Abs(-2.7), Math.Ceiling(2.7), and Math.Floor(2.7) is consistent; it does not vary.

```
Console.WriteLine(Math.Abs(-2.7)); // 2.7
Console.WriteLine(Math.Ceiling(2.7)); // 3
Console.WriteLine(Math.Floor(2.7)); // 2
```

E1.2

No. Consider a case when you remove (or rename) the directory. In this case, the same input will show you a different result because of the invalid path. In fact, any dependency on the external world can hamper the function's purity. Though in many cases, those situations are difficult to avoid.

E1.3

In many cases you cannot avoid using an impure function. But FP focuses on pure functions; so, our target will be to make a solution that closely matches the expectations. So, we can try to segregate the "pure" and "impure" parts. For example, you can isolate the I/O. (You will learn more about this when I discuss the Functional Core, Imperative Shell pattern.)

E1.4

"C# supports first-class functions." This indicates that you can treat functions like any other variables. For example, you can assign a function to a variable, treat it as an argument to another function, or use it as a return type. If you are familiar with Func (or Action) delegates or if you are a lambda lover, you are already familiar with the concept.

E1.5

Consider the following code:

```
static Func<int, int> GetSquareFunction()
{
    Func<int, int> squareFunction = x => x * x;
    return squareFunction;
    //return x => x * x;
}
```

You can see that the function named GetSquareFunction accepts nothing but returns a Func<int, int> type. The commented line shows that you can shorten the code length using a lambda expression too. Here is a sample program that uses this code:

```
using static System.Console;

WriteLine("Exercise 1.5 ");
int a = 10;
var square = GetSquareFunction();
WriteLine($"The square of {a} is: {square(a)}");
```

```
static Func<int, int> GetSquareFunction()
{
    Func<int, int> squareFunction = x => x * x;
    return squareFunction;
    //return x => x * x;
}
```

This program produces the following output:

```
Exercise 1.5
The square of 10 is: 100
```

Additional Note

Visual Studio IDE will suggest you use a local function in a similar context. It is also easy to understand. I have highlighted the change in bold (and kept the old code) for your easy understanding:

```
public static Func<int, int> GetSquareFunction()
{
  // Func<int, int> squareFunction = x => x * x;
    static int squareFunction(int x) => x * x;
    return addFunction;
}
```

Shortly, you'll understand that a local function is a functional programming feature. This feature allows you to use a function within another function. It makes your code clearer too. In addition, this prevents the function from being directly invoked from outside. Remember that function composition (discussed in the next chapter), clear readability, and immutability are common characteristics of FP.

E1.6

No. If a pure function depends on an impure function, it is no longer pure.

E1.7

Yes, it is possible. For example, an impure function that does the I/O can use the result obtained from a pure function. When given the same input, a pure function produces the same output; it is in no way related to the impurities.

E1.8

These are the pure functions:

```
public static int FindDifference(int a, int b)
{
  return Math.Abs(a - b);
}
public static int GetSquare(int x)
{
  return x * x;
}

internal double DividePositiveNumbers(PositiveNumber a,
  PositiveNumber b)
{
  return a.Number / b.Number;
}

public static int Get75()
{
  return 75;
}
```

The following functions are impure because you are mutating the state:

```
public static void ChangeStatus()
{
  OpsDone = !OpsDone;
}
```

```
public static int GetCube(int x)
{
 OpsDone = true;
 return x * x * x;
}
```

The following function is impure because it can raise an exception when b is 0.

```
public int Divide(int a, int b)
{
 return a / b;
}
```

The void return type of the following function already indicates that the function will do something, but it will not return anything. You may also notice that it is printing a message to the console and mutating the state. So, the function is indeed impure.

```
public void DoSomething(string input)
{
 WriteLine($"Doing some specific operation based on {input}.");
 OpsDone = true;
}
```

The following function is impure by nature:

```
public DateTime GetCurrentTime()
{
 return DateTime.Now;
}
```

You will notice a different output each time you call them. You can easily test this with the following code:

```
WriteLine(sample.GetCurrentTime());
Thread.Sleep(1000);
WriteLine(sample.GetCurrentTime());
```

CHAPTER 2

Understanding Functions

In the previous chapter, you saw a quick overview of functions and learned about pure functions versus impure functions. Since functions are the building blocks for FP, recognizing them and understanding their usage will make your functional journey easier. This is the reason we'll spend this whole chapter discussing different aspects of functions.

Mathematical Background of Functions

How are mathematics and computer science related to each other? There has been a long debate about this for years. The Department of Computer Science at the University of Oxford says the following (see `https://www.cs.ox.ac.uk/teaching/mcs/`):

> *Mathematics is a fundamental intellectual tool in computing, but computing is increasingly also a tool in mathematical problem solving.*

Although a strong foundation in mathematics is not necessary for students of computer science, I have found that much of the computing logic in programming can be easily understood if your mathematical foundation is strong. To illustrate this, I'll first discuss the mathematical background of functions. Later you'll see how that fits into C# programming.

In mathematics, a *function* is a rule or law that defines the relationship between two variables. Simply, it relates an input to an output. In 1837, the German mathematician Peter Dirichlet proposed the modern concept of a function $y = f(x)$ (pronounced as "f of x") saying the following:

> *If a variable y is so related to a variable x that whenever a numerical value is assigned to x, there is a rule according to which a unique value of y is determined, then y is said to be a function of the independent variable x.*

© Vaskaran Sarcar 2023
V. Sarcar, *Introducing Functional Programming Using C#*, https://doi.org/10.1007/978-1-4842-9697-4_2

In this context, you will often see three terms used: domain, range (or, image), and codomain. The set of all possible values of x is called the **domain** of the function, and the set of values of f(x) is called the **range** of the function. The **codomain** is the set of all possible outcomes of a given function. In other words, what can go into a function is called a *domain*, what can come out from a function is called a *codomain*, and what exactly comes out from a function is called the *range* of the function. It is interesting to note that though the codomain can be equal to the range of the function, in general, the range is the subset of the codomain.

Author's note   What is a set? It is a collection of things, such as numbers. For example, a set of even numbers looks like this: {...,-6,-4,-2,0,2,4,6,8,..}.

Imagine a function (let's call it **f**) mapping from positive numbers to positive numbers, as shown in Figure 2-1.

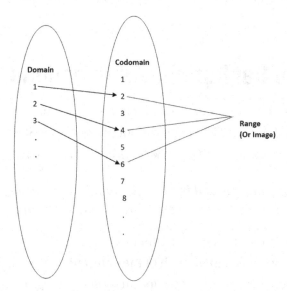

Figure 2-1.   *Domain, codomain, and range for a function mapping*

From Figure 2-1, you can see the following:

- *Domain set*: {1,2, 3, 4,5,6,...}

- *Range (or, image) set*: {2,4,6, ...}

- *Codomain set*: {1,2,3,4,5,6, ...}

Notice that the function **f** maps 1 to 2, 2 to 4, 3 to 6, and so on. In mathematics, you can write f(1)=2, f(2)=4, f(3)=6, and so on. Most importantly, following this pattern, you can understand that this example represents the function f(x)=2x where x is a positive number.

Now the question is, can you relate this to C# programming? Yes, you can. For example, you can use the int type for both the domain and the codomain in this example. So, a function can map int to int; simply, given an int, it produces an int.

Mathematical Functions vs. C# Functions

You should now have a basic idea what mathematical functions are. Are C# functions similar to them? Indeed, these mathematical functions are similar to the pure functions you saw in Chapter 1. In both cases, given an input, you get a consistent output.

But C# functions often perform critical jobs and talk to the outside world. In short, they can create side effects.

Representing Functions in C#

You can represent functions using any of the following constructs in C#:

- Methods

- Delegates

- Lambdas

- Dictionaries

Before we go into further detail, let's quickly review them. If you are familiar with them, you can skip to the next section; otherwise, continue reading and get a quick review.

To compare different representations, I'll write some simple programs that evaluate the function $f(x)=2x$. For simplicity, let's consider a domain set that contains the numbers 1 to 5.

Using Static Methods

Normally, a method is a code block with some statements (I am not talking about empty methods). These statements are placed together to do a specific task. Unlike C/ C++, they do not exist independently. Following the OOP style, typically they belong to some classes, and we call them **methods**. In Chapter 1, you have seen that these are nothing but functions.

Have you noticed the `System.Math` class? It includes methods for common mathematical functions. On further investigation, you'll notice that `Math` is a `static` class that contains many static methods. This gives you a clue how to organize pure functions in the functional style. In Demonstration 1, I'll also use static methods (aka static functions).

Demonstration 1

If you're an OOP programmer, the approach used in the following program will be familiar. Here I call the `DisplayNumbers` method to print a list of integers, and I invoke the `MultiplyEachElementByTwo` method to multiply each element of the list by 2. I am using a `foreach` loop to print these elements. Here is the complete program for you:

```
using static System.Console;

WriteLine("Evaluating the function: f(x)= 2x.");
List<int> domainSet = new() { 1, 2, 3, 4, 5 };
Write("Domain: [");
Helper.DisplayNumbers(domainSet);
Write("]");
WriteLine();

List<int> rangeSet = Helper.MultiplyEachElementByTwo(domainSet);
Write("Range: [");
Helper.DisplayNumbers(rangeSet);
WriteLine("]");

static class Helper
{
    public static void DisplayNumbers(List<int> numberList)
    {
        foreach (int i in numberList)
        {
            Write(i + "\t");
        }
    }
}
```

```
public static List<int> MultiplyEachElementByTwo(List<int>
 numberList)
{
    List<int> temp=new();
    foreach (int i in numberList)
    {
        temp.Add(i*2);
    }
    return temp;
}
}
```

Output

This code produces the following output:

```
Evaluating f(x)= 2x.
Domain: [1     2      3      4      5        ]
Range: [2      4      6      8      10       ]
```

Simplifying the Code

This program is easy to understand. Following functional programming, you can refactor the program and make it shorter. Here is a sample for you (notice the important changes in bold):

```
using static System.Console;
WriteLine("Evaluating the function: f(x)= 2x");

List<int> domainSet = Enumerable.Range(1, 5).ToList();
Write("Domain:[ ");
domainSet.ForEach(x => Write(x + "\t"));
Write("]");

WriteLine();

Write("\nRange:[ ");
domainSet.ForEach(x => Write(x * 2 + "\t"));
Write("]\n");
```

You can see that the following changes were made in this program:

- I used the built-in Range function to generate a list of numbers.

- I replaced the foreach loop using the ForEach function.

To use the Range function, I needed to pass the starting number and the count of numbers (which is 5 here). Since the Range function returns an IEnumerable<Int32> in C#, I used the ToList() function to convert this result into a list. This is because I wanted to use the ForEach function, which is available in the List<T> class. Then I replaced the foreach loop with the ForEach function. This is an extension method, and you'll find it beneficial. Later you'll learn that extension methods help you compose functions using method chaining, which increases the readability of the code and is very useful. You'll see a detailed discussion of this topic when I discuss method chaining and pipelining in Chapter 4.

Q&A Session

2.1 I see that you replaced the foreach loop with the ForEach function. Do you think ForEach is better than foreach?

No. In fact, foreach is probably more readable than ForEach. But I find ForEach helpful in certain scenarios.

First, you can reduce the code length. You saw an example of this when I used it in the previous program.

Second, once you start composing functions using method chaining, you'll find it is more readable at the end of a long chain. In fact, in the case of parallel programming, you may notice a similar coding style. For example, see the following code segments:

```
WriteLine("\nUsing Parallel.ForEach");
Parallel.ForEach(domainSet, x => Write(x + "\t"));
```

Or see the following code:

```
WriteLine("\nOdd numbers in the list are as follows:");
domainSet.Where(i => i % 2 != 0)
        .ToList()
        .AsParallel()
        .ForAll(x => Write(x + "\t"));
```

2.2 The ForEach function is defined in the List<T> class only. Similar support is not available for other data structures. So, it appears that its usage is limited. Is this correct?

You can define an extension method to provide similar support for other data structures as well. I'll show you an example in Demonstration 4 where I similarly traverse dictionary elements.

Using Delegates and Lambdas

Can we write an equivalent program using delegates? Surely, we can. In fact, the delegates and lambda expressions help you most in functional programming. Let's discuss them.

A Quick Review

Do you remember how the built-in delegates Func and Action work? Func has zero or more input parameters and one output parameter. The last parameter in the angle brackets, <>, is considered the return type, and the remaining parameters are considered input parameter types. For example, Func<int, int> tells that this delegate encapsulates a method that takes one input parameter of the int type and returns a value of the int type. So, you can assign any function to this delegate instance where the function takes one input parameter as an int and returns a value as an int.

Action is similar to Func except for the fact that it doesn't return a value. In other words, an Action delegate can be used with a method that has a void return type.

Let's evaluate function f(x)=2x again using delegates. This function takes an input and makes it two times bigger. So, I can write the following code when I return the computed result:

```
Func<int, int> multiplyByTwo = x =>
{
    return x * 2;
};
```

If you are familiar with lambda expressions, you can see that I have used the statement lambdas here. A **statement lambda** has a statement block as its body. But an **expression lambda** has an expression as its body, and it is very concise. You'll see the use of expression lambdas heavily in functional programming with C#. Using the expression lambda, we can write the following one-liner:

```
Func<int, int> multiplyByTwo = x => x * 2;
```

But if you use the Action delegate, you'll write something like the following (because in this case, you are working on a function that accepts an input but does not return anything):

```
public static Action<int> multiplyByTwo = x =>
{
    x *= 2;
    Write(x + "\t");
};
```

Alternatively, you can write something like the following:

```
Action<int> multiplyByTwo =  x => Write(x * 2 );
```

Note   Using the line using static System.Console; at the top of the file, I can use Write instead of Console.Write in the corresponding places.

Both of these code segments show that the multiplyByTwo represents the functionality where you pass an int. You then multiply this input by 2 and get another int.

Demonstration 2

You saw me using the ForEach function, but did you notice its signature? Here it is:

```
public void ForEach(Action<T> action);
```

You can see that `ForEach` expects you to pass an instance of the generic `Action` delegate. This is why in the following code I have used the `Action<int>` delegate but not the `Func<int>` delegate. Here is the complete program:

```
using static System.Console;

WriteLine("Evaluating f(x)= 2x using delegates.");
List<int> domainSet = new() { 1, 2, 3, 4, 5 };
Action<int> displayNumbers = x => Write(x + "\t");

Write("Domain: [");
// Passing the delegate as a function argument
domainSet.ForEach(displayNumbers);
Write("]");

WriteLine();

Action<int> multiplyByTwo = x => Write(x * 2 + "\t");
Write("Range: [");
// Passing the delegate as a function argument
domainSet.ForEach(multiplyByTwo);
WriteLine("]");
```

Output

This code produces the following output. It is the same except for the first line, which says that you are using delegates now.

```
Evaluating f(x)= 2x using delegates.
Domain: [1      2       3       4       5       ]
Range: [2       4       6       8       10      ]
```

Note   You have just started learning about functional programming. These are simple programs that focus on the key aspects of a topic that we discuss. Later you'll see that to make better programs, we'll separate data from the functions that do the actual computation.

Additional Note

Notice the following lines in this program:

```
Action<int> displayNumbers = x => Write(x + "\t");
// Passing the delegate as a function argument
domainSet.ForEach(displayNumbers);
```

In this example, I could produce the same output using lambdas only. I have not shown that here, because you have already seen that usage in Demonstration 1 that used the following line:

```
domainSet.ForEach(x => Write(x + "\t"));
```

Using a Dictionary

A dictionary is a common data structure. Microsoft says (see https://learn.microsoft.com/en-us/dotnet/api/system.collections.generic.dictionary-2?view=net-7.0) the following:

> The Dictionary<TKey,TValue> generic class provides a mapping from a set of keys to a set of values. Each addition to the dictionary consists of a value and its associated key.

A dictionary is a collection of key-value pairs. But we can represent functions using them. For example, think of a key as an element from a domain and the corresponding value as the range (or codomain). In that way, it acts like a function; in fact, it is a direct representation of this function where there is no computation involved. So, using a dictionary, you can represent any arbitrary function. For example, let's consider a function **f** where f(1)=1, f(2)=50, f(3)=42, f(4)=25, and so on.

Demonstration 3

We have been discussing the function f(x)=2x. Let's continue to represent the same function for the same domain set (the numbers from 1 to 5). Consider the following code:

```
using static System.Console;

WriteLine("Experimenting with an arbitrary function.");
```

```
Dictionary<int, int> multiplyByTwo = new()
{
    {1,2 },
    {2,4 },
    {3,6 },
    {4,8 },
    {5,10 }
};
for (int i = 1; i <= multiplyByTwo.Count; i++)
{
    WriteLine($"f({i})={multiplyByTwo[i]}");
}
```

Output

This code produces the following output:

```
Experimenting with an arbitrary function.
f(1)=2
f(2)=4
f(3)=6
f(4)=8
f(5)=10
```

Q&A Session

2.3 The ForEach function is defined in the List<T> class only. Earlier you said that we can define an extension method to provide similar support for other data structures. Can you show an example to traverse the dictionary elements?

Yes, the List<T> class has the ForEach function, but similar support is not available for other data structures. Using an extension method, you can introduce similar support for other sequences as well. The following demonstration will show you how.

Demonstration 4

The following program produces the same output as Demonstration 3:

```
using static System.Console;
using Extensions;

WriteLine("Experimenting with an arbitrary function!");
Dictionary<int, int> multiplyByTwo = new()
{
    {1,2 },
    {2,4 },
    {3,6 },
    {4,8 },
    {5,10 }
};
multiplyByTwo.ForEach(x =>
  WriteLine($"f({x.Key})={x.Value}"));

namespace Extensions
{
    public static class Extensions
    {
        public static void ForEach<T>(this IEnumerable<T>
          sequence, Action<T> action)
        {
            if (action != null)
            {
                foreach (T item in sequence)
                {
                    action(item);
                }
            }
        }
    }
}
```

Built-in Delegates Are Important

You have seen that C# functions can have various representations, but in the functional world, you'll notice delegates and lambdas are used in most places. Once you understand their usage, your functional journey will be easy.

- You can use custom delegates in your programs. But instead of using custom delegates, Microsoft recommends you use the built-in delegates such as Func or Action. These are generic delegates, and they have many overloaded versions. For example, at the time of this writing, there are 17 overloaded versions of the Func delegate. They can take 0 to 16 input parameters but always have one return type. They are as follows:

  ```
  Func<out TResult>
  Func<in T, out TResult>
  Func<in T1, in T2,out TResult>
  Func<in T1, in T2, in T3, out TResult>
  ......
  Func<in T1, in T2, in T3,in T4, in T5, in T6,in T7,in
    T8,in T9,in T10,in T11,in T12,in T13,in T14,in T15,in
    T16, out TResult>
  ```

- The Action delegates can be used for methods that can take arguments but have a void return type. What does this mean? A method that has a void return type normally causes side effects. Chapter 1 told you that functional programmers try to avoid side effects as much as possible. So, you'll normally prefer Func delegates over Action delegates.

- These built-in delegates will be sufficient to fulfill most of your needs. This is why understanding them can make your functional journey easy. **You'll also see me using the built-in delegates** Func **and** Action **heavily in this book.**

Higher-Order Function

In the previous chapter, I classified the functions based on purity, and you learned about pure functions and impure functions. In FP, you will also see terms like *first-order functions* and *higher-order functions*.

Treating functions as first-class citizens provides many benefits. HOF is one of them. A higher-order function is a function with any of the following characteristics:

- It takes one or more functions as input.

- It returns a function as output.

- It can do both.

You can use different C# constructs to make a HOF. Let's look at some examples.

Note   You know that if a language supports first-class functions, you can pass a function as an argument to another function, or you can use it as a return type. So, constructing an HOF is possible if you use a programming language that treats functions as first-class citizens.

Custom HOF

Let's experiment with some custom HOFs. The following code shows that the ShowSquare function accepts two parameters. You can see that one of these parameters is a Func<int, int> type. So, ShowSquare is an HOF.

```
static void ShowSquare(Func<int, int> func, int a)
{
    int result = func(a);
    WriteLine($"Square of {a} is: {result}");
}
```

To invoke this function, I can use the following lines in the client code:

```
int a = 10; ;
Func<int, int> squareFunction = x => x * x;
ShowSquare(squareFunction, a);
```

Notice that while invoking the function ShowSquare, I pass the delegate instance squareFunction to it.

In Demonstration 5, I'll use another function. Here it is:

```
static Func<int, int> MakeSquare()
{
    Func<int, int> squareFunction = x => x * x;
    return squareFunction;
}
```

You can see that the MakeSquare function accepts nothing but returns a Func<int, int> type. So, it is another example of an HOF.

Demonstration 5

You saw two HOFs. The following is a complete program that uses them:

```
using static System.Console;

WriteLine("Example of HOFs using Func delegate.");
int a = 10; ;
Func<int, int> squareFunction = x => x * x;
ShowSquare(squareFunction, a);

int result = MakeSquare()(a+2);
WriteLine($"The square of {a+2} is: {result}");

static void ShowSquare(Func<int, int> func, int a)
{
    int result = func(a);
    WriteLine($"The square of {a} is: {result}");
}
static Func<int, int> MakeSquare()
{
    Func<int, int> squareFunction = x => x * x;
    return squareFunction;
}
```

Output

This program will produce the following output:

```
Example of HOFs using Func delegate.
The square of 10 is: 100
The square of 12 is: 144
```

Additional Note

Once again, let me remind you that by using lambda expressions you can make the code shorter. For example, inside the MakeSquare function, you can replace the following lines with the line return x => x * x; to get the same output:

```
Func<int, int> squareFunction = x => x * x;
return squareFunction;
```

You may also note that the line Func<int, int> squareFunction = x => x * x; can be replaced with the following line (using a **local function**):

```
static int squareFunction(int x) => x * x;
```

Built-in HOF

Let's see a built-in HOF now. LINQ is an important part of C#, and it is functional by nature. LINQ users can easily find many functions that are higher-order ones.

Demonstration 6

Consider the following program:

```
using static System.Console;

var numbers = Enumerable.Range(1, 10);
WriteLine("Even numbers in the list are as follows:");
numbers.Where(i => i % 2 == 0)
      .ToList()
      .ForEach(x => Write(x + "\t"));
```

Output

It's easy to understand that this program finds even numbers from a given list. Here is the output:

```
Even numbers in the list are as follows:
2       4       6       8       10
```

Analysis

See the presence of the Where function in Demonstration 6. Let's investigate this function signature, which is as follows:

```
public static IEnumerable<TSource> Where<TSource>(
  this IEnumerable<TSource> source,
  Func<TSource, bool> predicate
);
```

You can see that this is an extension method that takes a function type (Func<TSource, bool>) as an argument. So, it is an HOF.

First-Order Function

Functions that are not HOF are called *first-order functions*. For example, a function that takes built-in data types such as an int and returns an int is an example of a first-order function.

Refactoring Impure Functions

You have seen different forms of functions and know that FP likes pure functions and avoids impure functions. So, let's discuss another important aspect when you need to refactor the impure functions to pure functions. In the upcoming section, I'll show you a simple refactor mechanism.

Program with Impurities

The following program uses a class `Transformer` that includes one constructor and one function. First, we'll try to analyze whether this function is impure. If you find that it is an impure function, your goal will be to refactor this program and convert the impure function to a pure function. Here are the important points in this program:

- The `Transformer` class has an instance method (aka function) called `MultiplyBy`. You can pass a number while invoking this method to get a new number.

- This new number is calculated based on a multiplication operation in which you multiply the input with a multiplier.

- When you can make an instance of this class, you pass a `double` type, which will act as a multiplier in this program.

Demonstration 7

Here is the complete program:

```
using static System.Console;
Transformer transformer = new(2);
var result = transformer.MultiplyBy(5.5);
WriteLine($"Result: {result}");
class Transformer
{
    double multiplier;
    public Transformer(double multiplier)
    {
        this.multiplier = multiplier;
    }
    public double MultiplyBy(double input)
    {
        return input * multiplier;
    }
}
```

Output

This program produces the following output, which is easy to understand:

```
Result: 11
```

Now can you tell me, is the function pure? It may appear to you that `transformer.MultiplyBy(5.5)` produces the same output as long as the multiplier is the same. But notice that this function can produce a different result if you instantiate a `Transformer` object with a different multiplier. FP programmers can find this immediately. They will immediately tell you that since you are working on the state (`multiplier` in this example), this function is impure.

Now the question is, can you make this function pure? Let's investigate.

Removing Impurities

As a first step toward functional programming, I'll make the function `MultipleBy` static. This time we'll also delete the instance state because the pure function will not work on it.

The built-in `System.Math` class in C# contains many pure functions. Following this class, we can make the `Transformer` class `static` too. But you may note that making the class `static` is optional in our case. It is because the criteria of a pure function are the following:

- A pure function does not change any data outside of the function.

- It has no side effects.

Since the function `MultiplyBy` is static, you can invoke this function without a `Transformer` instance. You'll pass both the input and the multiplier during this function invocation.

Demonstration 8

The following program demonstrates the sample program for you:

```
using static System.Console;
var result = Transformer.MultiplyBy(5.5, 2);
WriteLine($"Result: {result}");
```

```
static class Transformer
{
    public static double MultiplyBy(
     double input, double multiplier)
    {
        return input * multiplier;
    }
}
```

Output

You can see that this refactored version also produces the same output.

```
Result: 11
```

Additional Note

I have demonstrated a simple example; you may not see the immediate benefits from this refactored code. As you progress more with FP, you'll discover this refactor mechanism is useful for other complex programs as well.

Q&A Session

2.4 You are using the line using static System.Console; for all demonstrations in this chapter. Is there any reason for this?

C# 6 introduced this feature. This statement allows you to import all the static members of a type. As a result, you can write cleaner code without further qualification. FP likes pure functions because you can reason and test them in isolation. This is one of the primary reasons a functional library in C# mainly contains static functions (aka methods). So, using static statements are pretty helpful when you consume a functional library and write cleaner code.

Author's note The using static statement operates a little differently with extension methods. If interested, you can learn more about it at https://learn.microsoft.com/en-us/xamarin/cross-platform/platform/csharp-six.

2.5 By using such statements are you polluting namespaces?

Good question. Yes, overusing such statements will surely lead to namespace pollution, but reasonable use of them seems good to me. Clean code not only helps you, but it also helps others as well.

We have covered many important aspects of functions in this chapter. You can complete the following exercises and move to the next chapter.

Exercises

E2.1 Can you write a program using an HOF that has a parameter of the following type?

```
Action<int, int>
```

E2.2 Is the following function an HOF? If so, can you write a sample program using it?

```
static Action<int, int> GetTotalMaker()
{
    Action<int, int> total =
     (x, y) => WriteLine($"{x}+{y}={x + y}");
    return total;
}
```

E2.3 Can you predict the output of the following code?

```
using static System.Console;
var numbers = Enumerable.Range(10, 7).ToList();
Func<int, bool> isEven = x => x % 2 == 0;
numbers.Where(isEven)
       .ToList()
       .ForEach(x => WriteLine(x));
```

E2.4 In Exercise 2.3, given a list of numbers, you retrieved the even numbers. In other words, you picked a list of numbers that are divisible by 2. In this context, can you show the use of an HOF to find the list of numbers where these numbers are divisible by an arbitrary number (such as 2, 3, or 5) that you choose?

E2.5 Identify the first-order and higher-order functions in the following program. Can you predict the output?

```
using static System.Console;
WriteLine("Exercise 2.5");
Func<int, int> triple = x => x * 3;
Action<Func<int,int>, int> tripleMaker = ( Func<int, int> f, int
  x ) =>
{
    WriteLine($"Triple of {x} is: {f(x)} ");
};
tripleMaker(triple,10);
```

E2.6 Identify the first-order and higher-order functions in the following program. Can you predict the output?

```
using static System.Console;

WriteLine("Exercise 2.6");
Action<int, int> add =
    (x, y) => WriteLine($"{x} + {y} = {x + y}");
Func<Action<int, int>> makeTotal = () =>
{
    WriteLine("The makeTotal function is called.");
    return add;
};
makeTotal()(10, 15);
```

Summary

Functions are the building blocks for FP. This chapter included a detailed discussion of them. Specifically, it covered the following topics:

- How are mathematical functions related to C# functions?

- How can you represent functions in C#?

- What are first-order functions?

- What are higher-order functions?

- How can you represent an HOF in C#?

- How can you use a local function in C#?

- How can you refactor an impure function to a pure function?

Solutions to Exercises

Here are the solutions.

E2.1

Here is a sample program:

```
using static System.Console;

WriteLine("Using a HOF that has an Action<int,int> parameter.");
int a = 10, b = 5;
Action<int, int> add= (x, y) => WriteLine($"{x}+{y}={x + y}");
DisplayTotal(add,a,b);
static void DisplayTotal(Action<int, int> del, int a,int b)
{
    del(a,b);
}
```

It produces the following output:

```
Using a HOF that has an Action<int, int> parameter.
10+5=15
```

E2.2

Yes. Here is a sample program:

```
using static System.Console;

WriteLine("Using a HOF that returns an Action<int, int> ");
int a = 20, b = 7;
```

```
Action<int, int> result = GetTotalMaker();
result(a,b);

static Action<int, int> GetTotalMaker()
{
    Action<int, int> total =
     (x, y) => WriteLine($"{x}+{y}= {x + y}");
    return total;
}
```

It produces the following output:

```
Using a HOF that returns an Action<int, int>
20+7= 27
```

Author's note You can make a shorter form of the program as follows (notice the key changes in bold):

```
using static System.Console;

WriteLine("Example 2.2: Using a HOF that has the return type
 Action<int, int> ");
int a = 20, b = 7;
```

GetTotalMaker()(a,b);

```
static Action<int, int> GetTotalMaker()
{
    return (x, y) => WriteLine($"{x}+{y}= {x + y}");
}
```

E2.3

This program picks the even numbers between 10 and 17:

```
10
12
14
16
```

E2.4

Here is a sample program that shows multipliers of 2, 3, and 5 (between 10 and 17) using an HOF:

```
using static System.Console;
var numbers = Enumerable.Range(10, 7).ToList();
Func<int, bool> isMod(int n) => x => x % n == 0;
WriteLine("Multipliers of 2(Even Numbers):");
numbers.Where(isMod(2))
        .ToList()
        .ForEach(WriteLine);

WriteLine("Multipliers of 3:");
numbers.Where(isMod(3))
        .ToList()
        .ForEach(WriteLine);

WriteLine("Multipliers of 5:");
numbers.Where(isMod(5))
        .ToList()
        .ForEach(WriteLine);
```

Here is the output of the program:

```
Multipliers of 2(Even Numbers):
10
12
14
16
Multipliers of 3:
12
15
Multipliers of 5:
10
15
```

E2.5

In this program, `triple` is a variable of type `Func<int, int>`. It holds a first-order function that is expressed with the lambda expression `x => x * 3;`. Similarly, the `tripleMaker` variable holds the HOF, which is represented by another lambda expression. This HOF accepts the first-order function `triple`. Here is the output of the program:

```
Exercise 2.5
Triple of 10 is: 30
```

E2.6

In this program, the `add` variable acts as the first-order function. Similarly, `makeTotal` is the HOF that accepts first-order function `add`. Here is the output of the program:

```
Exercise 2.6
The makeTotal function is called.
10 + 15 = 25
```

Additional Note

You may note that, in this program, the following line:

```
makeTotal()(10, 15);
```

is a simplified form for the following lines:

```
Action<int, int> action = makeTotal();
action(10, 15);
```

CHAPTER 3

Understanding Immutability

Functional programming uses immutability to improve code quality and understandability. Chapter 1 offered a brief overview of immutability, and this chapter will go into depth on this topic. It will also present some case studies.

What Is Immutability?

According to Google, immutability means "unchanging over time" or "unable to be changed." So, the immutable types are objects (or data structures) that are not changeable. You may ask, does this mean they are not changeable after creation or not changeable after certain phases? There are different variations of immutability, which we will cover in this chapter. But let's start with reviewing the concept of .NET objects.

Immutable Objects in .NET

Objects are the foundation of traditional object-oriented programs. What is an object? Basically, it is an instance of a class. Each object has two parts: state and behavior. The behaviors of an object are modeled by methods. And what about the state? It is represented by the values of an object's fields. For an immutable object, the state should not be changed once the initialization process ends. So, **in the .NET world, we call a type *immutable* if it does not change its internal state once it is initialized.**

I'll discuss different types of immutability in this chapter. It is a big topic, and all the concepts may not be straightforward. The goal of this chapter is to make the overall concept simpler for you. Basically, in an immutable program, the program components remain the same over time. More simply, an immutable object should not change over time.

59

© Vaskaran Sarcar 2023
V. Sarcar, *Introducing Functional Programming Using C#*, https://doi.org/10.1007/978-1-4842-9697-4_3

POINT TO NOTE

The Microsoft documentation (`https://learn.microsoft.com/en-us/archive/msdn-magazine/2017/march/net-framework-immutable-collections`) says the following:

Considering that F# is a functional-first language, all instances are immutable unless explicitly specified otherwise. On the other hand, C# is an object-oriented first language in which all instances are mutable unless explicitly specified otherwise.

So, to make a type immutable in C#, you need to do some "additional coding." As you progress on this chapter, you'll find some interesting techniques to do this.

Q&A Session

3.1 Why is immutability preferred in FP?

The Microsoft documentation (see `https://learn.microsoft.com/en-us/archive/msdn-magazine/2017/march/net-framework-immutable-collections`) states it nicely.

> *The fundamental benefit of immutability is that it makes it significantly easier to reason about how the code works, enabling you to quickly write correct and elegant code.*

In fact, the advantages of immutable types are apparent once you see their basic characteristics. Since immutable types are not changeable after creation, they are thread-safe, and they help you avoid side effects. Avoiding side effects is important because you know that they make the code difficult to understand, and often, they compromise the code quality. On the contrary, the absence of side effects improves code readability.

In short, FP likes immutability because it matches the philosophy that the state (or data) of a running program should not change over time.

3.2 Why does FP worry about state mutations?

Allowing state mutations can complicate a program. For example, consider the case of a concurrent update that can lead to a race condition. This kind of situation is difficult to reproduce and test. Also, debugging such a scenario is tough.

In addition, once you're more familiar with FP, you can avoid many unintended couplings in your code if you restrict the state mutations.

Reviewing Mutable Types

Before we work on immutable types, it'll be helpful to understand their counterpart: mutable types. Reviewing mutable types can help you understand the changes that are necessary to make a type immutable.

Programming with a Mutable Type

In the following program, you'll see the presence of the Employee class. This class has two properties: a Name and an Id. You can guess that these properties are used to represent the name and ID (an identification number) of an employee. Your job is to identify whether Employee is an immutable type.

Demonstration 1

Let's run the following code and then look at the output:

```
using static System.Console;

WriteLine("Understanding Mutability.");
Employee emp1 = new("Sam", 1);
WriteLine(emp1);
// Setting the new ID for emp1
emp1.Id = 2;
WriteLine(emp1);

class Employee
{
    public string Name { get; set; }
    public int Id { get; set; }
    public Employee(string name, int id)
    {
        Name = name;
        Id = id;
    }

    public override string ToString() =>
     $"Name: {Name}, ID: {Id}";
}
```

Output

This program produces the following output:

```
Understanding Mutability.
Name: Sam, ID: 1
Name: Sam, ID: 2
```

Analysis

The output shows that though emp1 was initialized with the name Sam and ID 1, later the ID is changed to 2. So, it is clear that Employee is a mutable type.

Now the question is: can you refactor this code to make the Employee type immutable?

The Path Toward Immutability

To make the Employee type immutable, we need to work on its properties. In C#, the string type is already immutable. So, to make the Employee type immutable, you need to focus on its Id property. But instead of focusing only on the Id property, in general, as a first step toward immutability, let's make the setters private. This can prevent the client code from directly modifying an Employee instance.

Achieving External Immutability

Consider the following code with the key changes in bold:

```csharp
class Employee
{
    public string Name { get; private set; }
    public int Id { get; private set; }

    public Employee(string name, int id)
    {
        Name = name;
        Id = id;
    }
```

```
public override string ToString() =>
  $"Name: {Name}, ID: {Id}";
}
```

This time, the following code (notice the bold line) does not compile:

```
using static System.Console;
Employee emp1 = new("Sam", 1);
WriteLine(emp1);
emp1.Id = 2; // Error CS0272
WriteLine(emp1);
```

You will see the following compile-time error:

```
CS0272    The property or indexer 'Employee.Id' cannot be used in this
context because the set accessor is inaccessible
```

If you want to change the ID that is associated with the name Sam, you can make a new Employee instance as follows:

```
// To change Sam's ID, we need to create a new object
emp1 = new("Sam", 2);
```

So, how can we distinguish this new employee instance from the previous one (since we used the common variable name emp1)? We can compare the corresponding hash codes.

Demonstration 2

Here is a complete demonstration for you. To preserve the initial hash code, I created a temporary variable called temp. Later I used this variable to compare the variable with the new hash code.

```
using static System.Console;

WriteLine("Understanding Mutability and Immutability.");
Employee emp1 = new("Sam", 1);
WriteLine(emp1);
//emp1.Id = 2; // Error CS0272
Employee temp = emp1;
```

```
WriteLine($"The emp1's hashcode:{emp1.GetHashCode()}");
WriteLine($"The temp's hashcode:{temp.GetHashCode()}");

// To change Sam's ID, we create a new object
emp1 = new("Sam", 2);
WriteLine(emp1);
WriteLine($"The emp1's hashcode:{emp1.GetHashCode()}");
WriteLine($"The temp's hashcode:{temp.GetHashCode()}");
class Employee
{
    public string Name { get; private set; }
    public int Id { get; private set; }

    public Employee(string name, int id)
    {
        Name = name;
        Id = id;
    }

    public override string ToString() =>
      $"Name: {Name}, ID: {Id}";

}
```

Output

Here is a sample output (the hash code can be different on your computer):

```
Understanding Mutability and Immutability.
Name: Sam, ID:1
The emp1's hashcode:43942917
The temp's hashcode:43942917
Name: Sam, ID:2
The emp1's hashcode:59941933
The temp's hashcode:43942917
```

Since the external code cannot change the properties anymore, the Employee type is **externally immutable**.

Enforcing Internal Immutability

Let's add an instance method called SetNewId to the Employee class as follows (notice the change in bold):

```
class Employee
{
    public string Name { get; private set; }
    public int Id { get; private set; }

    public Employee(string name, int id)
    {
        Name = name;
        Id = id;
    }
    public void SetNewId(int id)
    {
        Id = id;
    }
    public override string ToString() =>
      $"Name: {Name}, ID: {Id}";
}
```

Can you tell me whether the Employee type is immutable now? Initially, the type seems to be immutable because the following code will not compile:

```
using static System.Console;
Employee emp1 = new("Sam", 1);
WriteLine(emp1);
emp1.Id = 2; // Error CS0272
```

But notice that this time you expose a new method SetNewId, and the type becomes mutable again. Invoking this method, a client can change the Id property again. Now you understand that the type is mutable from the inside.

This scenario depicts the fact that if a developer adds a new method to an existing immutable type without careful analysis, the type can mutate its internal states. In our example, after the addition of the SetNewId method, the Employee type has lost its external immutability too.

What is the solution? You can use read-only properties from the beginning. Look at the following program with the important changes in bold:

```
class Employee
{
    public string Name { get; }
    public int Id { get; }

    public Employee(string name, int id)
    {
        Name = name;
        Id = id;
    }
    //public void SetNewId(int id)
    //{
    //     Id = id; // Error CS0200
    //}
    public override string ToString()
    {
        return $"Name: {Name}, ID:{Id}";
    }
}
```

In this case, if you try to expose the method SetNewId (as shown in the commented code), you'll receive the following compile-time error:

```
CS0200    Property or indexer 'Employee.Id' cannot be assigned to -- it is
read only
```

This solves one part of the problem. **Now the question is, can we use the SetNewId method without breaking the immutability?** Yes, we can. Consider the following code:

```
public Employee SetNewId(int id)
{
  // Creating a new object with
  // existing name and supplied id
  return new Employee(Name,id);
}
```

The supporting comment shows that you can create a new Employee object keeping the current name of the employee with an Id change. Most importantly, the Employee type is still immutable.

If you need to work on this type, you'll discover that the type is **internally immutable**. It is unlikely that without sufficient reasons and discussions with the team members, you'd make the type mutable again.

Demonstration 3

The following program demonstrates the concept I just discussed:

```
using static System.Console;

WriteLine("Achieving Internal Immutability.");
Employee emp1 = new("Sam", 1);
// emp1.Id = 2; // Error Now
Employee emp2 = emp1.SetNewId(2); // OK

WriteLine($"Emp1: {emp1}");
WriteLine($"Emp2: {emp2}");

class Employee
{
    public string Name { get; }
    public int Id { get; }

    public Employee(string name, int id)
    {
        Name = name;
        Id = id;
    }
    public Employee SetNewId(int id)
    {
        // Creating a new object with an
        // existing name and supplied id
        return new Employee(Name, id);
    }
}
```

```
    public override string ToString() =>
        $"Name: {Name}, ID: {Id}";

}
```

Output

This program produces the following output:

```
Achieving Internal Immutability.
Emp1: Name: Sam, ID:1
Emp2: Name: Sam, ID:2
```

Better Code Using Modern Features

If you carefully investigate the previous scenario, you'll understand that the addition of SetNewId to the Employee type was needed to create a new Employee instance keeping the same name, but with a different ID. So, can you write better code to keep the Employee type immutable? I think you can. Continue reading.

Let's refactor the code. This time I'd like to use some useful features, such as record, the with expression, and the init accessor, which have been available since **C# 9.0**. In the context of immutability, these are very useful. Let's see what Microsoft says about them (https://learn.microsoft.com/en-us/dotnet/csharp/language-reference/builtin-types/record).

> *Beginning with C# 9, you use the record keyword to define a reference type that provides built-in functionality for encapsulating data. C# 10 allows the record class syntax as a synonym to clarify a reference type, and record struct to define a value type with similar functionality. You can create record types with immutable properties by using positional parameters or standard property syntax.*

POINTS TO REMEMBER

This quote makes two important points.

- While records can be mutable, they're primarily intended for supporting immutable data models.

- A `record` or a `record class` declares a reference type. The `class` keyword is optional but can add clarity for readers. A `record struct` declares a value type.

In this chapter, we started our discussion with `class`, so let's focus on `record class`.

Let's investigate the other feature called the `with` expression now. Microsoft (`https://learn.microsoft.com/en-us/dotnet/csharp/language-reference/operators/with-expression`) says the following:

Available in C# 9.0 and later, a with expression produces a copy of its operand with the specified properties and fields modified.

It continues as follows:

In C# 9.0, a left-hand operand of a with expression must be of a record type. Beginning with C# 10, a left-hand operand of a with expression can also be of a structure type or an anonymous type.

Now the question is, how can you implement the modifications? You can use object initializer syntax to specify the intended with their new values. Here is a sample with supporting comments:

```
// Original instance
Employee emp1 = new("Sam", 1);
// Creating a new instance keeping the same
// name, but modifying the ID
Employee emp2 = emp1 with { Id = 2};
```

About the init accessor Microsoft (https://learn.microsoft.com/en-us/dotnet/csharp/language-reference/keywords/init) says the following:

In C# 9 and later, the init keyword defines an accessor method in a property or indexer. An init-only setter assigns a value to the property or the indexer element only during object construction. This enforces immutability, so that once the object is initialized, it can't be changed again.

Demonstration 4

All these features are easy to understand. Let's examine them in the following program:

```
using static System.Console;
WriteLine("Use of record type, init accessor, and with Expression.");
Employee emp1 = new("Sam", 1);
var emp2 = emp1 with { Id = 2};

WriteLine($"Emp1: {emp1}");
WriteLine($"Emp2: {emp2}");

record class Employee
{
    public string Name { get; init; }
    public int Id { get; init; }

    public Employee(string name, int id)
    {
        Name = name;
        Id = id;
    }
    public override string ToString() =>
      $"Name: {Name}, ID: {Id}";

}
```

Output

This program produces the following output:

```
Use of record type, init accessor, and with expression.
Emp1: Name: Sam, ID: 1
Emp2: Name: Sam, ID: 2
```

Note   As discussed, you can use the GetHashCode method to verify that these objects (emp1 and emp2) are different. This means the immutability is preserved.

Q&A Session

3.3 Suppose I have the following code. Is the Employee type immutable?

```
class Employee
{
    public string Name { get; }
    public int Id { get; }

    public Employee(string name, int id)
    {
        Name = name;
        Id = id;
    }
    public override string ToString()
    {
        return $"Name: {Name}, ID:{Id}";
    }
}
```

Yes.

3.4 I am confused. I see that when you initialize an object of `Employee` (shown in Q&A 3.3), you need to supply the values for the `Name` and `Id` properties. In such a case, you are reassigning the default values. Does this not go against the principle of FP?

Nice observation. Yes, to make an `Employee` object, you must initialize it first. But see what Microsoft says the following about it (`https://learn.microsoft.com/en-us/archive/msdn-magazine/2017/march/net-framework-immutable-collections`).

> *Technically, there are many kinds of immutability. Any type that somewhat restricts changes to its state or the state of its instances can be described as immutable in some sense.*

The `Employee` type in Q3.3 can be considered immutable because once it's initialized, you cannot change the name or ID of an employee. For your immediate reference, you can consider the following code that produces compile-time errors (shown in bold):

```
Employee emp = new ("Sam", 1);
emp.Name = "Jack"; // Error CS0200
emp.Id = 2; // Error CS0200
```

3.5 I have found that updating data is often required in certain programs. But my understanding is that immutability opposes the idea. How can I deal with a similar situation if I prefer immutability?

Certain C# features can help you in a similar context. You saw the use of the `with` expression in Demonstration 4. But, in most cases, you'll notice a common pattern that is as follows: you create a new object with the intended updates and use this new object in those places where you need to use the updated values. (In Exercise E3.4, I have provided a sample solution in a similar context.)

More on Immutability

You have learned about external immutability and internal immutability. I told you earlier that immutability is a big topic. So, there are many interesting case studies. In the upcoming section, you will see some of them.

Understanding Shallow Immutability

In Demonstration 5, you'll see two classes: Employee and Department. The second one is used to form a department using the Employee instances. Your job is to analyze whether these types are immutable. If not, you must make them immutable.

First, look at the Employee type, which is as follows:

```
class Employee
{
    public string Name { get; }
    public int Id { get; }

    public Employee(string name, int id)
    {
        Name = name;
        Id = id;
    }
    public override string ToString() =>
      $"Name: {Name}, ID: {Id}";

}
```

You can see that the Name and Id properties inside the Employee class are read-only. You can supply the corresponding values when you instantiate an Employee only. This is why you know that the Employee type is immutable.

Now let's look at the other class. Let's assume that to form a department with one or more employees someone has written the following code:

```
class Department
{
    public string Name { get; }
    public List<Employee> Employees { get; }
    public Department(string name, List<Employee> emps)
    {
        Name = name;
        Employees= emps;
    }
}
```

Is Department immutable? Let's analyze this.

You can see that Name is a string-type property. This means it is immutable. But what about Employees? It may appear that once assigned, the value of this field cannot be changed. To some extent, this is a correct observation. For example, in the following code segment:

```
using static System.Console;
List<Employee> mathEmployees = new()
{
    new("Sam", 1),
    new("Bob", 2)
};

Department mathDept = new("Mathematics", mathEmployees);
WriteLine($"Employee count:{mathDept.Employees.Count}");
mathDept.Name = "Physics"; // Error CS0200
mathDept.Employees = null; //  Error CS0200
```

you will observe the following errors:

```
CS0200    Property or indexer 'Department.Name' cannot be assigned to -- it
is read only
CS0200    Property or indexer 'Department.Employees' cannot be assigned
to -- it is read only
```

But notice that you can write the following code, which does not show any compile-time errors:

```
mathDept.Employees.Add(new("Jack", 3)); // OK
```

Not only that, the following line of code can compile too:

```
mathEmployees.Add(new("Kate", 4)); // Also OK
```

Since you can add new employees to the initial employee list (mathEmployees), you can change mathDept. You have seen that though you cannot mutate mathDept directly, you can mutate it indirectly through mathEmployees. This is an example of **shallow immutability**.

Demonstration 5

It is time for a complete demonstration that shows everything we have discussed in this section. Here is the complete program with supporting comments for your reference:

```csharp
using static System.Console;
WriteLine("Understanding Shallow Immutability.");
List<Employee> mathEmployees = new()
{
    new("Sam", 1),
    new("Bob", 2)
};

Department mathDept = new("Mathematics", mathEmployees);
WriteLine($"Employee count:{mathDept.Employees.Count}");
// We cannot mutate the state directly,
// but we can do the same using
// the Employees property

// mathDept.Name = "Physics"; // Error CS0200
// mathDept.Employees = null; //  Error CS0200
mathDept.Employees.Add(new("Jack", 3)); // OK
WriteLine($"Employee count:{mathDept.Employees.Count}");
mathEmployees.Add(new("Kate", 4)); // Also OK
WriteLine($"Employee count:{mathDept.Employees.Count}");

class Employee
{
    public string Name { get; }
    public int Id { get; }
    public Employee(string name, int id)
    {
        Name = name;
        Id = id;
    }
    public override string ToString() =>
     $"Name: {Name}, ID: {Id}";
```

```
}
class Department
{
    public string Name { get; }
    public List<Employee> Employees { get; }
    public Department(string name, List<Employee> emps)
    {
        Name = name;
        Employees= emps;
    }
}
```

Output

This program produces the following output:

```
Understanding Shallow Immutability.
Employee count:2
Employee count:3
Employee count:4
```

Analysis

You have seen that Department is immutable only to some extent. Though we made the Employees property read-only, Department is not completely immutable. You cannot change the department name or employee details for mathDept (which is an instance of Department) directly, but you can incorporate a change indirectly when you use any of the following lines:

```
mathDept.Employees.Add(new("Jack", 3));
mathEmployees.Add(new("Kate", 4));
```

In this example, the Employees property inside the Department class is a reference to the list instance, but C# lists are mutable. This was the root of the problem.

Searching for a Solution

Can you improve this situation? Yes, you can. In the previous section, you saw that there are multiple ways to update the employee list and change the Department instance (mathDept). To preserve the initial list of employees and make the Department class immutable, you have to prevent those updates. So, let me show you another version of Department, which will be used in the upcoming demonstration (I have commented out the old code for your reference):

```
class Department
{
    public string Name { get; }
    // public List<Employee> Employees { get; }
    public IReadOnlyCollection<Employee> Employees { get; }
    public Department(
      string name,
      IReadOnlyCollection<Employee> emps)
      {
        Name = name;
        Employees = emps;
      }
}
```

You can see that instead of List<Employee>, this time I have used IReadOnlyCollect ion<Employee>. What is the benefit? Now a client cannot use any of the following lines:

```
mathDept.Name = "Physics"; // Error CS0200
mathDept.Employees = null; //  Error CS0200
mathDept.Employees.Add(new("Jack", 3)); // Error CS1061
```

Most importantly, the last line of this code segment shows you the compile-time error.

```
CS1061    'IReadOnlyCollection<Employee>' does not contain a definition for
'Add' and no accessible extension method 'Add'
accepting a first argument of type 'IReadOnlyCollection<Employee>' could be
found (are you missing a using directive or an assembly reference?)
```

This means we have improved the situation from the perspective of making the type immutable. Still, there is a problem. Why? The following line still shows no compile-time error:

```
mathEmployees.Add(new("Kate", 4));
```

Let's verify this fact in Demonstration 6.

Demonstration 6

It is time for another complete demonstration that shows everything we have discussed in this section. Here is the complete program with supporting comments (notice the important changes in bold):

```
using static System.Console;
WriteLine("Improving the shallow immutability( Demo 7)");
List<Employee> mathEmployees = new()
{
    new("Sam", 1),
    new("Bob", 2)
};

Department mathDept = new("Mathematics", mathEmployees);
WriteLine($"Employee count:{mathDept.Employees.Count}");

// We cannot mutate the state directly
// mathDept.Name = "Physics"; // Error CS0200
// mathDept.Employees = null; //  Error CS0200

// Now the following line will raise a compile-time error
// mathDept.Employees.Add(new("Jack", 3)); // Error 1061 now

// Still, the following line shows no compile-time error
mathEmployees.Add(new("Kate", 4));
WriteLine($"Employee count:{mathDept.Employees.Count}");

class Employee
{
    public string Name { get; }
    public int Id { get; }
```

```csharp
    public Employee(string name, int id)
    {
        Name = name;
        Id = id;
    }
    public override string ToString() =>
     $"Name: {Name}, ID: {Id}";

}
class Department
{
    public string Name { get; }
    public IReadOnlyCollection<Employee> Employees { get; }
    public Department(string name, IReadOnlyCollection<Employee> emps)
    {
        Name = name;
        Employees = emps;
    }
}
```

Output

This program produces the following output:

```
Improving the shallow immutability.
Employee count:2
Employee count:3
```

Analysis

We have improved the situation, but the output shows that a client can still change the employee count through a specific operation. Let's continue our search for a better solution.

Making a Better Solution

Initially, I started with a List<Employee>. Later I used IReadOnlyCollection<Emplo yee>. But you can see that I need further improvements to make the Department type immutable. Let's try the following one (I have commented out the old code for your reference):

```
class Department
{
    public string Name { get; }
    // public List<Employee> Employees { get; }
    // public IReadOnlyCollection<Employee> Employees { get; }
    public ImmutableList<Employee> Employees { get; }
    public Department(string name, ImmutableList<Employee> emps)
      {
        Name = name;
        Employees = emps;
      }
}
```

This can solve the previous problems that you saw in Demonstration 5 and Demonstration 6. We will verify this with client code. But before that, let me tell you about the following points:

- ToImmutableList<TSource>(IEnumerable<TSource>) is an extension method that enumerates a sequence and produces an immutable list of its contents.

- When you add or remove items from an immutable list, a copy of the original list is made with the items added or removed, and the original list is unchanged.

Demonstration 7

Let's verify these facts with the following program where I have marked the important segments in bold:

```
using static System.Console;
using System.Collections.Immutable;

WriteLine("Improving the shallow immutability using an immutable list.)");
List<Employee> mathEmployees = new()
{
    new("Sam", 1),
    new("Bob", 2)
};

var immutableMathEmployees = mathEmployees.ToImmutableList();
WriteLine($"Initial count in the immutable
  list:{immutableMathEmployees.Count}"); // 2
WriteLine($"Forming the Math department with an immutable list
  of employees.");
Department mathDept = new("Mathematics",
  immutableMathEmployees);
WriteLine($"Employee count in the Math
  department:{mathDept.Employees.Count}"); // 2

// We cannot mutate the state directly,
// mathDept.Name = "Physics"; // Error CS0200
// mathDept.Employees = null; //  Error CS0200

WriteLine($"Adding Jack to the Math department");
Department updatedMathDept= new("Mathematics",
  mathDept.Employees.Add(new("Jack", 3)));
WriteLine($"Employee count in new
  department:{updatedMathDept.Employees.Count}");

WriteLine($"Adding Kate to the initial list.");
var updatedMathEmployees=
  immutableMathEmployees.Add(new("Kate", 4));
WriteLine($"Employee count in the updated
  list:{updatedMathEmployees.Count}");

WriteLine($"Employee count:{mathDept.Employees.Count}");
WriteLine($"Employee count:{immutableMathEmployees.Count}");
```

```csharp
class Employee
{
    public string Name { get; }
    public int Id { get; }

    public Employee(string name, int id)
    {
        Name = name;
        Id = id;
    }
    public override string ToString() =>
     $"Name: {Name}, ID: {Id}";

}
class Department
{
    public string Name { get; }
    public ImmutableList<Employee> Employees { get; }
    public Department (string name,
     ImmutableList<Employee> emps)
      {
        Name = name;
        Employees = emps;
      }
}
```

Output

When you run this program, you'll see the following output:

```
Improving the shallow immutability using an immutable list.
Initial count in the immutable list:2
Forming the Math department with an immutable list of employees.
Employee count in the Math department:2
Adding Jack to the Math department
Employee count in new department:3
Adding Kate to the initial list.
```

```
Employee count in the updated list:3
Employee count:2
Employee count:2
```

Analysis

The last two lines of output show that the initial employee list is unaffected in between operations. So, from the perspective of immutability, we have made a better version of the Department type.

Implementing Popsicle Immutability

There are some special cases where slightly weakening the write-once immutability is permissible and treated as a valid scenario. This is a special type of immutability; see Eric Lippert's blog post about it:

https://ericlippert.com/2007/11/13/immutability-in-c-part-one-kinds-of-immutability/

POINT TO NOTE

You may notice the terminology difference among the developers. For example, Microsoft says (https://devblogs.microsoft.com/premier-developer/read-only-frozen-and-immutable-collections/) that a collection or type is freezable if it is:

mutable until some point in time when it is frozen, after which it cannot be changed.

The overall idea will be clearer with a real-world example.

Have you heard of extempore speech competitions? In my school days, they were popular events. A student picks a paper from a box at random. Each paper contains a topic. The student then gives a talk on this topic to an audience. Presenting a topic without any proper preparation to an audience is an extraordinary capability.

But a student may pick a topic that they know nothing about. So, the school implemented a rule: you can pick a maximum of three papers, but you have to present your lecture based on the slip that you picked last. In other words, you cannot say that the previous paper had a better topic than the current one. It was both fun and exciting!

You can implement the same idea in programming. Suppose I have given you a constraint saying that you can change the ID of an employee, but you cannot do it more than a specified limit. Can you write a program for this?

Demonstration 8

The following program demonstrates the idea.

Note   I use raw string literals in the following program. This is not mandatory, but I want you to be familiar with this C# 11 feature. You can learn more about it at `https://learn.microsoft.com/en-us/dotnet/csharp/language-reference/proposals/csharp-11.0/raw-string-literal`.

```
using static System.Console;
WriteLine("Exploring the popsicle immutability.");
Employee emp = new("Sam", 1);
WriteLine($"Employee detail: {emp}");
emp.Id = 2; // OK
WriteLine($"Employee detail: {emp}");
emp.Id = 3; // No Change
WriteLine($"Employee detail: {emp}");
emp.Id = 4; // No Change
WriteLine($"Employee detail: {emp}");

class Employee
{
    public string Name { get; }
    private int id;
    private static int AttemptToIdChanged = 1;
    public int Id
    {
        get
        {
            return id;
        }
```

```
        set
        {
            if (AttemptToIdChanged < 3)
            {
                id = value;
                WriteLine($"The employee's ID is created.");
            }
            else
            {
                WriteLine($"""
                 The ID cannot be changed.
                 (Maximum limit is reached).
                 You tried {AttemptToIdChanged} times.
                 """);
            }
            AttemptToIdChanged++;
        }
    }

    public Employee(string name, int id)
    {
        Name = name;
        Id = id;
    }
    public override string ToString() =>
     $"Name: {Name}, ID: {Id}\n";

}
```

Output

Let's run this program and see the output:

```
Exploring the popsicle immutability.
The employee's ID is created.
Employee detail: Name: Sam, ID: 1
```

```
The employee's ID is created.
Employee detail: Name: Sam, ID: 2

The ID cannot be changed.
(Maximum limit is reached.)
You tried 3 times.
Employee detail: Name: Sam, ID: 2

The ID cannot be changed.
(Maximum limit is reached.)
You tried 4 times.
Employee detail: Name: Sam, ID: 2
```

Analysis

You can see that this program does not allow a client to change the employee's ID more than a specified limit, and it preserves the last ID that was set during a valid attempt.

Q&A Session

3.6 Are there any common guidelines to make an immutable type in C#?

Making immutable types is becoming easier with modern features. You saw them earlier in this chapter. Over the years engineers have found some useful techniques. Some of them are listed here:

- Consider making a sealed class.

- Use read-only properties (and avoid setters). You have seen me using get-only accessors heavily in this chapter. It is interesting to note that before C# 6, to make a read-only property, developers used a read-only backing field and initialized it in the constructor. But the introduction of get-only accessors makes the programming easy.

- Try making instance methods (aka functions) pure.

- Pay special attention to impure functions. You can make them static or refactor the code. For example, you can separate them into another type or do something more meaningful. Consider the cases with void methods. In general, they have side effects. So, you can try to minimize those effects. (In Exercise 3.4, you'll see a sample where

I refactor existing code by creating a new object with the intended updates. Then I use this new object in those places where I need to use the updated values.)

Exercises

E3.1 True or false? An immutable type does not change its internal state once it is initialized.

E3.2 Can you give some examples of built-in immutable types in C#?

E3.3 Can you predict the output of the following code and determine whether `Circle` is an immutable type?

```
using static System.Console;
Circle circle = new(7.5, "Red");
WriteLine($"Current detail: {circle}");
circle.IncrementRadiusBy(2);
WriteLine($"Current detail: {circle}");
class Circle
{
    public double Radius { get; set; }
    public string Color { get; set; }
    public Circle(double radius,string color)
    {
        Radius = radius;
        Color = color;
    }
    public void IncrementRadiusBy(int r)
    {
        Radius += r;
    }

    public override string ToString()=>
        $"Radius:{Radius} units, Color: {Color}";
}
```

E3.4 If you think that `Circle` is a mutable type in the previous question (E3.3), how can you make it immutable?

E3.5 Consider the following code. Do you consider `FifaTitles` to be an immutable type?

```
sealed class FifaTitles
{
  public string Name { get; }
  public Dictionary<string, int> CountriesWithNumbers
  {
   get;
  }
  public FifaTitles(string name,Dictionary<string, int>
   winners)
   {
     Name = name;
     CountriesWithNumbers = winners;
   }
}
```

Summary

This chapter discussed different facets of immutability with case studies. Briefly, it answered the following questions:

- What is immutability? Why is it helpful?

- What is an immutable type in .NET?

- What does a mutable type look like? Why are state mutations challenging in certain scenarios?

- What are the different forms of immutability?

- How do the modern C# features promote immutability?

- How can you refactor code to convert a mutable type to an immutable type?

And many more.

Solutions to Exercises

Here are the solutions.

E3.1

In general, the statement is true. But you saw the example of popsicle immutability where you are allowed to mutate a value to some extent. In this case, this statement is not 100 percent true.

E3.2

`System.String` and `System.MulticastDelegate` are two common examples of built-in immutable types in C#. The same is true for numbers as well as the null value.

E3.3

This program produces the following output:

```
Current detail: Radius:7.5 units, Color: Red
Current detail: Radius:9.5 units, Color: Red
```

You can see that this program allows you to modify the radius of an existing `Circle` instance. So, `Circle` is not immutable here.

E3.4

The following program shows a sample usage of the immutable version of `Circle` (notice the important changes in bold):

```
using static System.Console;
Circle circle = new(7.5, "Red");
WriteLine($"Current detail: {circle}");
Circle updatedCircle=circle.IncrementRadiusBy(2);
WriteLine($"Current detail: {updatedCircle}");
```

```
class Circle
{
    public double Radius { get; set; }
    public string Color { get; set; }
    public Circle(double radius, string color)
    {
        Radius = radius;
        Color = color;
    }

    public Circle IncrementRadiusBy(int r)
    {
        return new Circle(Radius + r, Color);
    }

    public override string ToString() =>
     $"Radius:{Radius} units, Color: {Color}";
}
```

This program also produces the same output you saw in E3.3.

E3.5

The `FifaTitle` is immutable to some extent because the following code will not work (errors are shown in bold):

```
using static System.Console;
WriteLine("Exercise 3.5");
Dictionary<string, int> worldCupRecords = new()
{
    {"Brazil",5 },
    {"Italy",4 },
    {"Germany",4 }
};

FifaTitles winners = new("MaximumTitleWinners", worldCupRecords);
WriteLine($"Current count: {winners.CountriesWithNumbers.Count}");
```

```
// We cannot mutate the state directly
winners.Name = "Atleast Four time winners"; // Error CS0200
winners.CountriesWithNumbers = null; // Error CS0200
```

However, it is not 100 percent immutable because the following lines will not cause any compile-time error:

```
// But we can mutate the state
// using the CountriesWithNumbers property

winners.CountriesWithNumbers.Add("Argentina", 3); // OK
WriteLine($"Current count: {winners.CountriesWithNumbers.Count}"); // OK
```

So, you can see that you can update the elements of the dictionary element, which is an instance of FifaTitles.

Author's note You can download the sample program (Exercise 3.5) from the Apress website.

PART II

Harnessing the Power of Functional Programming

C# is a multiparadigm language, and Part II reveals its potential. This part consists of six chapters. Here is a summary of what the chapters cover:

- **Chapter 4** explains function composition techniques using pipelining, and higher-order functions.

- **Chapter 5** explains function composition techniques using currying.

- **Chapter 6** discusses how to handle temporal couplings.

- **Chapter 7** introduces some functional patterns (such as Map, Bind, Filter, and Fold) using some core functions with simple examples.

- **Chapter 8** covers functional error-handling mechanisms.

- **Chapter 9** shows helpful C# features for functional programming. It includes a discussion of monads and wraps up by providing some useful tips that were not discussed in earlier chapters.

You should know that C# is primarily an object-oriented programming language. So, from a functional programmer's point of view, there is a big gap of specific functionalities that can be filled by using third-party libraries. I'll use two well-known external libraries, called Curryfy and language-ext, in this book. Curryfy will be used in Chapter 5 when I discuss currying, and language-ext will be used in Chapter 8 and Chapter 9 when I discuss functional error handling and the Monad pattern. You can harness these libraries to make better applications.

Author's note Developers often use language-ext and LanguageExt interchangeably. Remember that name of the library is "language-ext". But while programming, we use the namespace "LanguageExt".

CHAPTER 4

Composing Functions Using Pipelining

Understanding the building blocks of functional programming (FP) is essential. But using them effectively is equally important. Composing functions is an integral part of FP. This chapter discusses this topic.

Overview

Composing functions means combining multiple functions into a new function.

In mathematics, function composition is an operation o that takes two functions, f and g, and produces a function h = f o g such that h(x) = f(g(x)). In this example, the function f is applied to the result of applying the function g to x. The notation f o g is often read as "f of g," "f after g," "f following g," and so on. But the most important point is that you are working on a new function h that is a composition of f and g. As a result, applying h to a value x is the same as applying g to that same value x to obtain an intermediate result and then applying f to that intermediate result.

Coding Functional Composition

This chapter focuses on functional composition using pipelining, which is nothing but a compositional pattern. You will notice this pattern heavily in functional programming. Demonstration 3 of this chapter shows an example of pipelining. There you will see the use of the three integer variables a, b, and c in the following code:

```
result = Sample.Sum(a, b)
             .IsGreater(c);
```

© Vaskaran Sarcar 2023
V. Sarcar, *Introducing Functional Programming Using C#*, https://doi.org/10.1007/978-1-4842-9697-4_4

This code is used to verify whether the total of a and b is greater than c. You can identify the following benefits using this approach:

- Anyone who reads this can assume what it is trying to do. So, it is expressive enough.

- The sequence of these operations follows our natural way of reading. For example, you calculate the sum of the numbers, and then you start analyzing whether it is a greater number.

But there are alternative ways to compute the same result. For example, given the following code:

```
Func<int,int,int> add = (x,y) => x + y;
Func<int, int, bool> isGreater = (x, y) => x > y;
```

you can write something like the following to obtain the same result:

```
bool result2 = isGreater(add(a, b), c);
```

Notice that add is applied first and isGreater is applied after this function, but you are reading them in the reverse direction. Here I show you two functions only. What will happen if you have more functions? Obviously, reading more functions in the opposite direction will make the code harder to read.

Now you understand that the pipelining pattern improves the code readability. But before you learn this pattern, I will talk about chaining functions and the use of extension methods.

Author's note You know that OOP developers like to use the term *method* instead of *function*. So, they use the term *method chaining* to indicate chaining functions. In fact, I have seen developers use the term *method chaining, function chaining, functional method chaining,* or *fluent API* in a similar context. In every case, the essence is the same: they are talking about chaining some functions (aka methods), and you invoke these functions without using temporary variables.

Q&A Session

4.1 This chapter focuses on functional composition using pipelining with examples. Are there other techniques for functional compositions?

Yes. You can compose functions in different ways.

- You can make a higher-order function (HOF).

- You can use pipelining.

- You can use currying.

Each technique has its pros and cons. But probably pipelining outclasses the other techniques in C#. In fact, if you ask C# developers, they will probably say they prefer pipelining. So, I have started the discussion of functional composition by using pipelining. I discuss currying in Chapter 5. Also, HOFs are not new to you. You saw the uses of HOFs in Chapter 2 when we covered different aspects of functions.

4.2 What are the benefits of functional composition?

Instead of calling individual functions in a particular order, you can directly invoke the composed function to get the result. Combining these functions can provide many other benefits such as cleaner code and better readability. In Chapter 5, you will see that if a function has multiple parameters, by applying the currying technique, you can partially invoke the function even if all the required parameters are not available at the time of the function invocation. For example, instead of invoking the function $f(a,b,c)$, you can invoke it as $f(a)(b)(c)$.

4.3 Why do I need to be familiar with chaining functions (or, method chaining) before I learn pipelining?

Anyone who is familiar with method chaining understands that pipelining is nothing but a fancy term used in the programming world. Here we form a chain of functions where the output of one function becomes the input of the next function, and you continue the process.

4.4 Why do I need to know about extension methods before I learn about function composition?

This chapter focuses on functional composition using pipelining. You have seen that the pipelining pattern preserves the natural way of reading and helps you write cleaner code. A functional language like F# probably understands this benefit, which is why it already has a pipe operator (|) to provide support in a similar context. But C# is primarily an object-oriented language, and at the time of this writing, there is no such operator yet.

In addition, suppose you make a type that is already in the production code and customers are familiar with it. Later you want to enhance the capability without breaking the existing functionalities. In such cases, extension methods provide a great value. Let's see what Microsoft (`https://learn.microsoft.com/en-us/dotnet/csharp/programming-guide/classes-and-structs/extension-methods`) says about them.

> *Extension methods enable you to "add" methods to existing types without creating a new derived type, recompiling, or otherwise modifying the original type. Extension methods are static methods, but they're called as if they were instance methods on the extended type.*

The last line of the previous code indicates that after putting a dot, you can see the available extension method, which provides great help to the developers. For example, in Demonstration 3 of this chapter, I use the extension method `IsGreater`. I can see its presence after calling a compatible method (`Sum` in this case) and putting a dot, as shown in Figure 4-1.

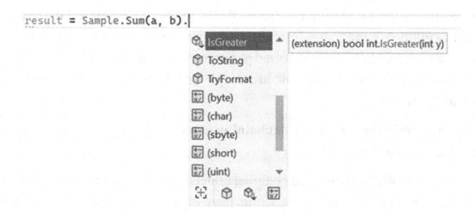

Figure 4-1. *Sample use of an extension method (IsGreater) that is used in Demonstration 3*

Now you understand that I can chain this extension method to serve my purpose. In short, chaining functions and using extension methods help you implement the pipeline pattern.

Finally, I assume you are aware of the functional nature of LINQ in C#. Often you use the standard query operators (such as select, where, etc.) and chain them. Upon investigation, you'll understand that these are extension methods. In Chapter 2 we investigated the Where function signature, which is as follows:

```
public static IEnumerable<TSource> Where<TSource>(
  this IEnumerable<TSource> source,
  Func<TSource, bool> predicate
);
```

You can see that this is an HOF because it has a function (Func<TSource, bool>) type parameter. But notice that it is also an extension method for the type IEnumerable<TSource>.

Importance of Chaining Functions

Often, we understand the usefulness of a technique in the absence of it. The usefulness of chaining functions is apparent once you see a program that does not use the technique. So, we will start our discussion with a program that does not chain functions.

Program Without Chaining Functions

In this section you will see a PcAssembler class that is used to assemble a personal computer (PC). To make things simple, let's make the following assumptions:

- There are three important activities: configuring the motherboard, configuring the central processing unit (CPU), and configuring the rest of the PC.

- This is why you'll see three functions (ConfigureMotherboard(), ConfigureCpu(), and AddOtherParts()) inside the PcAssembler class. I have used only console statements inside these functions to make things easy. Here is a sample:

  ```
  public void ConfigureMotherboard()
  {
   WriteLine("The motherboard is added.");
   IsMotherboardReady = true;
  }
  ```

- In addition, there are three properties: IsMotherboardReady, IsCpuReady, and IsOtherpartsReady. As per their names, you can assume that these properties are used to check whether the motherboard, CPU, and remaining parts are already assembled.

- When all these three parts are completed, the PC is completely assembled. I've overridden the ToString() method to display whether a particular instance of PcAssembler is completely assembled. So, the following code should make sense to you (do not worry, we'll give it a functional look shortly):

```
public override string ToString()
{
 if (IsMotherboardReady
  && IsCpuReady
  && IsOtherpartsReady)
 {
  return " The PC is complete now.";
 }
 else
 {
  return " The PC is not ready yet.";
 }
}
```

Demonstration 1

Here is the complete program. This program does not chain the corresponding functions.

```
using static System.Console;

WriteLine("Assembling a PC.");
PcAssembler assembler = new(false, false, false);
assembler.ConfigureMotherboard();
assembler.ConfigureCpu();
assembler.AddOtherParts();
WriteLine(assembler);
```

```
class PcAssembler
{
    bool IsMotherboardReady { get; set; }
    bool IsCpuReady { get; set; }
    bool IsOtherpartsReady { get; set; }
    public PcAssembler(bool motherBoard,
                       bool cpu,
                       bool otherParts)
    {
        IsMotherboardReady = motherBoard;
        IsCpuReady = cpu;
        IsOtherpartsReady = otherParts;
    }
    public void ConfigureMotherboard()
    {
        WriteLine("The motherboard is added.");
        IsMotherboardReady = true;
    }
    public void ConfigureCpu()
    {
        WriteLine("The CPU is configured.");
        IsCpuReady = true;
    }
    public void AddOtherParts()
    {
        WriteLine("All parts(except the CPU and motherboard)
         are configured.");
        IsOtherpartsReady = true;
    }
    public override string ToString()
    {
        if (IsMotherboardReady
            && IsCpuReady
            && IsOtherpartsReady)
```

```
        {
            return "The PC is complete now.";
        }
        else
        {
            return "The PC is not ready yet.";
        }
    }
}
```

Output

Here is the output of the program:

```
Assembling a PC.
The motherboard is added.
The CPU is configured.
All parts(except the CPU and motherboard) are configured.
The PC is complete now.
```

Analysis

Now I have the following questions for you:

- Did you notice that PcAssembler is not immutable?

- An assembler can vary the steps; for example, someone may want to work on CPU configuration before working on the motherboard and vice versa. Can you add this flexibility to your program?

See the next program.

Refactoring Using Chaining Functions

The upcoming program uses the concept of chaining functions and makes your code more readable. The following code block demonstrates that initially the PC was not ready; then you configure a motherboard, then you configure the CPU, and finally you join other parts together:

```
PcAssembler assembler = new PcAssembler(false, false, false)
                        .ConfigureMotherboard()
                        .ConfigureCpu()
                        .AddOtherParts();
```

In the same way, if you see the following code:

```
PcAssembler assembler = new PcAssembler(false, false, false)
                        .ConfigureCpu()
                        .ConfigureMotherboard()
                        .AddOtherParts();
```

you can easily assume that the assembler works on the CPU before working on the motherboard. This technique is known as **method chaining**.

Note   Method chaining is a technique in which functions (aka methods) are called on in sequence to form a chain, and each of these functions returns an instance of a class. You chain these functions together to form a single statement and make your code more readable.

To implement this concept of chaining functions, you need to work on the PcAssembler class and change the return types of these methods. Here is a sample:

```
public PcAssembler ConfigureMotherboard()
{
  WriteLine("The motherboard is added.");
  return new PcAssembler(true, IsCpuReady, IsOtherpartsReady);
}
```

The return statement in the previous function supports immutability, which is another important aspect of functional programming. Let's make the PcAssembler class immutable also by removing the setters as follows:

```
bool IsMotherboardReady { get; }
bool IsCpuReady { get; }
bool IsOtherpartsReady { get; }
```

Finally, the Visual Studio IDE wants you to avoid if-else statements and suggests converting it into a conditional expression. You also know that the functional world wants you to use expressions instead of statements. So, this time I refactor the ToString method as follows:

```
public override string ToString() =>
    IsMotherboardReady
    && IsCpuReady
    && IsOtherpartsReady
        ? "The PC is complete now."
        : "The PC is not ready yet.";
```

Demonstration 2

To demonstrate everything we have discussed so far, the following program is ready for you:

```
using static System.Console;
WriteLine("Assembling a PC. (Using method chaining.)");

PcAssembler assembler = new PcAssembler(false, false, false)
                            .ConfigureMotherboard()
                            .ConfigureCpu()
                            .AddOtherParts();
WriteLine(assembler);
class PcAssembler
{
    bool IsMotherboardReady { get; }
    bool IsCpuReady { get; }
    bool IsOtherpartsReady { get; }
    public PcAssembler(bool motherBoard,
                    bool cpu, bool otherParts)
    {
        IsMotherboardReady = motherBoard;
        IsCpuReady = cpu;
        IsOtherpartsReady = otherParts;
    }
```

```csharp
public PcAssembler ConfigureMotherboard()
{
    WriteLine("Motherboard is added.");
    return new PcAssembler(true, IsCpuReady,
      IsOtherpartsReady);
}
public PcAssembler ConfigureCpu()
{
    WriteLine("The CPU is configured.");
    return new PcAssembler(IsMotherboardReady, true,
      IsOtherpartsReady);
}
public PcAssembler AddOtherParts()
{
    WriteLine("All parts(except the CPU and motherboard)
      are configured.");
    return new PcAssembler(IsMotherboardReady, IsCpuReady,
      true);
}
public override string ToString() =>
    IsMotherboardReady
    && IsCpuReady
    && IsOtherpartsReady
        ? "The PC is complete now."
        : "The PC is not ready yet.";

}
```

Output

Here is the output of the program:

```
Assembling a PC. (Using method chaining.)
The motherboard is added.
The CPU is configured.
All parts(except the CPU and motherboard) are configured.
The PC is complete now.
```

Applying Composition

Once you are familiar with chaining functions (aka method chaining), you will realize that pipelining is basically an implementation of method chaining. In the case of pipelining, you will deal with multiple functions in such a way that the output of the first function becomes the input of the next function, and so forth.

Using Pipelining

Let's look at a demo application that matches the definition of pipelining.

Demonstration 3

In the following demonstration, the Sample class has a method called Sum that takes two integers as input and returns the total.

```
static class Sample
{
    public static int Sum(int x, int y) => x + y;
}
```

Let's assume you want to verify whether the sum of these numbers is greater than another given number. For example, the sum of 10 and 20 is greater than 25. To test this programmatically, you can introduce an extension method as follows:

```
public static bool IsGreater(this int x, int y) => x > y;
```

To test that the sum of 10 and 20 is greater than 25, a client can write the following code now:

```
int a=10, b=20, c=25;
var result = Sample.Sum(a, b)
                    .IsGreater(c);
```

Here is a demonstration:

```
using ExtLibrary;
using static System.Console;
```

```
WriteLine("Experimenting pipelining.");
int a=10, b=20, c=25;

var result = Sample.Sum(a, b)
                    .IsGreater(c);
WriteLine($"Is {a}+{b} greater than {c}? {result}");

// Testing new values
a = 25;
b = 45;
c = 100;

result = Sample.Sum(a, b)
                .IsGreater(c);
WriteLine($"Is {a}+{b} greater than {c}? {result}");

static class Sample
{
    public static int Sum(int x, int y) => x + y;

}
namespace ExtLibrary
{
 public static class Extensions
  {
    public static bool IsGreater(this int x, int y) => x > y;
  }
}
```

Note   In this program, the extension method resides in the same file. But did
you notice that I used a different namespace for the extension method? This
is because, in common practice, we create extension methods in the other
assemblies (we call them *class libraries*). Following this approach, you can reuse
an extension method in different projects.

Output

Here is the output of the program:

```
Experimenting pipelining.
Is 10+20 greater than 25? True
Is 25+45 greater than 100? False
```

Analysis

Look at the following code segment one more time:

```
int a=10, b=20, c=25;
var result = Sample.Sum(a, b)
                    .IsGreater(c);
```

You can see that this is easily understandable. Anyone who reads this code can assume that in the first step, you are making a total of two integers, and in the next step, you are compare them with another integer.

This concept is not new, and I assume that you have used it many times with built-in constructs in C#. For example, you can use a `StringBuilder` instance and use different functions one by one such as the following:

```
using System.Text;
using static System.Console;

StringBuilder builder = new("Hello, ");
int length = builder.Append("reader! How are you")
                    .Insert(builder.Length, "?")
                    .Length;
WriteLine($"The string is: {builder}");
WriteLine($"Its length is: {length}");
```

This code produces the following output:

```
The string is: Hello, reader! How are you?
Its length is: 27
```

LINQ users are very much used to this technique. Here is the sample code:

```
using static System.Console;
List<int> numbers = new() { 10, 21, 6, 14, 9 };
WriteLine("Even numbers in increasing order:");
numbers.Where(i => i % 2 == 0)
       .OrderBy(x => x)
       .ToList()
       .ForEach(WriteLine);
```

This produces the following output:

```
Even numbers in increasing order:
6
10
14
```

You can see that this code uses the extension methods- Where, OrderBy and the concept of method chaining.

Q&A Session

4.5 In Demonstration 3, you showed an example of function composition using the pipelining pattern. Can you show an equivalent program using HOFs?

Since I discussed HOFs in Chapter 2, I have not repeated the material here. You can look at Demonstration 4, which will produce function composition using HOFs.

Using HOFs

In the following program, I'll use a function called Compose. It is also an extension method and is defined as follows:

```
public static Func<int, int, int, bool> Compose(
 this Func<int, int, int> func1,
 Func<int, int, bool> func2)
  {
    return (x, y, z) => func2(func1(x, y), z);
  }
```

Here are two important observations:

- This function accepts a function parameter and returns a function type.

- Notice the function body. It has two functions where func1 is applied before func2.

Let's see the usage of the Compose function in Demonstration 4.

Demonstration 4

Here is the complete program:

```
using ExtLibrary;
using static System.Console;

WriteLine("Composing functions using HOF.");
Func<int,int, int> sum = (x, y) => x + y;
Func<int, int, bool> isGreater = (x, y) => x > y;

var composedFunc = sum.Compose(isGreater);
int a = 10, b = 20, c = 25;
bool result = composedFunc(a,b,c);
WriteLine($"Is {a}+{b} greater than {c}? {result}");

// Testing new values
a = 25;
b = 45;
c = 100;
result = composedFunc(a, b, c);
WriteLine($"Is {a}+{b} greater than {c}? {result}");

static class Sample
{
    public static int Sum(int x, int y)
    {
        return x + y;
    }

}
```

```
namespace ExtLibrary
{
    public static class Extensions
    {
        public static Func<int,int,int,bool> Compose(
          this Func<int, int, int> func1,
          Func<int,int,bool> func2)
          {
            return (x, y, z) => func2(func1(x, y), z);
          }

    }
}
```

Output

This program produces the same output except for the first line, which states that this time you are using an HOF:

```
Composing functions using HOF.
Is 10+20 greater than 25? True
Is 25+45 greater than 100? False
```

Analysis

In this demonstration, you can use a lambda expression when you compose the functions. For example, the following line in Demonstration 4:

```
var composedFunc = sum2.Compose(isGreater2);
```

can be replaced with the following line:

```
var composedFunc = sum2.Compose((x, y) => x > y);
```

In fact, you can use the generic version of the Compose function as follows:

```
public static Func<T,T,T,bool> GenericCompose<T>(
  this Func<T,T,T> func1,
  Func<T, T,bool> func2) where T : struct
```

```
{
  return (x, y, z) => func2(func1(x, y), z);
}
```

Q&A Session

4.6 Demonstration 3 and Demonstration 4 show the same output. Which one do you prefer?

Though we are achieving the same result, I prefer pipelining over HOF. For me, pipelining provides better readability.

Exercises

E4.1 True or false? Pipelining is a compositional pattern where the output of the first function becomes the input of the next function and the chain grows like this.

E4.2 Suppose you are composing multiple functions using pipelining and there is a function that matches the Action<int> type. Can you place this function in the middle of a chain?

E4.3 Consider the following program and predict the output:

```
Func<int, int, int> makeTotal = (x, y) => x + y;
Func<int, int> makeCube = x => x * x * x;
int tempResult = makeTotal(2, 3);
int finalResult= makeCube(tempResult);
WriteLine($"Result: {finalResult}");
```

This program follows an imperative style of coding. Can you compose the functions using an HOF and rewrite the program to make it functional?

E4.4 Consider the code segment shown in E4.3. Can you compose the functions using pipelining and rewrite the program to make it functional?

E4.5 Demonstration 2 was a modified version of Demonstration 1. There you made your code more readable, applied the concept of method chaining, and made the PcAssembler class immutable. Following the functional paradigm, can you enhance the implementation considering a new requirement that demands you display the service charge once the assembler completes its job?

You do not need to write separate unit tests for this program. It will be sufficient to show one positive use case (the PC is assembled completely) and one negative use case (the PC is not ready).

Summary

This chapter discussed functional composition and answered the following questions:

- What is meant by functional composition?

- What are the benefits of functional composition?

- What are the different types of composition?

- How can you use the concept of method chaining?

- How can you use compose functions using pipelining?

- How can you compose functions using HOFs?

Solutions to Exercises

Here are the solutions.

E4.1

True.

E4.2

No. An Action delegate (and its overloaded forms) is used for functions with the void return type. The functions that can be represented by Action delegates can appear only at the end of the chain.

E4.3

This program produces the following output:

Result: 125

The following program demonstrates the use of an HOF and produces the same output:

```
using FpLibrary;
using static System.Console;

WriteLine("Exercise 4.3");
Func<int, int, int> makeTotal = (x, y) => x + y;
Func<int, int> makeCube = x => x * x * x;
// Using HOF
var combinedFunc = makeTotal.Compose(makeCube);
var result = combinedFunc(2, 3);
WriteLine($"Result: {result}");

namespace FpLibrary
{
    public static class Extensions
    {
        public static Func<int, int, int> Compose(
            this Func<int, int, int> total,
            Func<int, int> cube)
        {
            return (x, y) => cube(total(x, y));
        }
    }
}
```

As usual, instead of using the nongeneric Compose function, you can use the generic version as follows:

```
// Generic Version
 public static Func<T,T,T> GenericCompose<T>(
  this Func<T,T,T> total,
```

```
Func<T,T> cube)
{
 return (x, y) => cube(total(x,y));
}
```

Or, you can make it more concise as follows:

```
public static Func<T, T, T> GenericCompose<T>(
  this Func<T, T, T> total,Func<T, T> cube) =>
   (x, y) => cube(total(x, y));
```

E4.4

The following program demonstrates the use of the pipelining pattern and produces the same output:

```
using FpLibrary;
using static System.Console;

WriteLine("Exercise 4.4");
// Using pipeline pattern
var result = 2.MakeTotal(3)
                 .MakeCube();
WriteLine($"Result: {result}");

namespace FpLibrary
{
    public static class Extensions
    {

      public static int MakeTotal(this int a, int b) => a + b;
      public static int MakeCube(this int a) => a * a * a;

    }
}
```

E4.5

Do you introduce a new function inside PcAssembler? If you think like this, let me bring the following points to your attention:

- Suppose this PcAssembler is written by a third party and you do not have direct access to the code. In this case, you cannot introduce this new function inside the PcAssembler.

- When you introduce a function inside an existing class, you violate one of the core principles, called the Open/Closed principle.

Is there any better solution? I think so. See the following program, which uses an extension method:

```
static class PcAssemblerExtention
    {
        public static PcAssembler GetServiceCharge(this
          PcAssembler assembler)
        {
            WriteLine("Service charge is generated.");
            return assembler;
        }
    }
```

Here is the complete demonstration:

```
using Extentions;
using static System.Console;

WriteLine("Exercise 4.5");

WriteLine("Use case-1:");
PcAssembler assembler = new PcAssembler(false, false, false)
                        .ConfigureMotherboard()
                        .ConfigureCpu()
                        .AddOtherParts()
                        .GetServiceCharge();
WriteLine(assembler);
```

```
WriteLine("\nUse case-2:");
assembler = new PcAssembler(false, false, false)
                .ConfigureCpu()
                .AddOtherParts()
                .GetServiceCharge();
WriteLine(assembler);
class PcAssembler
{
    bool IsMotherboardReady { get; }
    bool IsCpuReady { get; }
    bool IsOtherpartsReady { get; }
    public PcAssembler(bool motherBoard,
                       bool cpu,
                       bool otherParts)
    {
        IsMotherboardReady = motherBoard;
        IsCpuReady = cpu;
        IsOtherpartsReady = otherParts;
    }
    public PcAssembler ConfigureMotherboard()
    {
        WriteLine("The motherboard is added.");
        return new PcAssembler(true, IsCpuReady,
          IsOtherpartsReady);
    }
    public PcAssembler ConfigureCpu()
    {
        WriteLine("The CPU is configured.");
        return new PcAssembler(IsMotherboardReady, true,
          IsOtherpartsReady);
    }
    public PcAssembler AddOtherParts()
    {
        WriteLine("All parts(except the CPU and motherboard)
          are configured.");
        return new PcAssembler(IsMotherboardReady, IsCpuReady,
```

```
                    true);
    }
    public override string ToString() =>
       IsMotherboardReady
       && IsCpuReady
       && IsOtherpartsReady
          ? "The PC is complete now."
          : "The PC is not ready yet.";

}
namespace Extentions
{
    static class PcAssemblerExtention
    {
        public static PcAssembler GetServiceCharge(this
          PcAssembler assembler)
        {
            WriteLine("A service charge is generated.");
            return assembler;
        }
    }
}
```

Here is the output of the program:

```
Exercise 4.5
Use case-1:
The motherboard is added.
The CPU is configured.
All parts(except the CPU and motherboard) are configured.
A service charge is generated.
The PC is complete now.

Use case-2:
The CPU is configured.
All parts(except the CPU and motherboard) are configured.
A service charge is generated.
The PC is not ready yet.
```

118

CHAPTER 5

Composing Functions Using Currying

In the previous chapter, you learned about function composition using pipelining. You reviewed function composition using higher-order functions (HOFs) too. Now I'll show you one more technique, called *currying*, which is not common in OOP development. It is common in functional programming, though. If you are learning about currying for the first time, you may find it difficult to understand. But once you grasp the basic concepts, you'll value the effort. Like the previous chapters, the goal of this chapter is to simplify the concept with easy-to-understand examples.

Overview of Currying

Suppose you have a function that has n (where n>1) number of parameters. To invoke this function in the traditional way, you must supply the corresponding n number of arguments. You cannot invoke the function without those n arguments. But currying provides you with some flexibility. It allows you to invoke this function with one argument and get back a function that will wait for the remaining arguments. And you continue the process until you pass all the arguments.

Note Wikipedia (see `https://en.wikipedia.org/wiki/Currying`) describes this nicely by saying the following: "In mathematics and computer science, currying is the technique of translating the evaluation of a function that takes multiple arguments into evaluating a sequence of functions, each with a single argument."

© Vaskaran Sarcar 2023
V. Sarcar, *Introducing Functional Programming Using C#*, https://doi.org/10.1007/978-1-4842-9697-4_5

In the previous chapter, to show you the importance of chaining functions, I started with a program that did not chain functions. I will follow the same approach in this chapter. Before I tell you more about currying, I will show you a sample program that does not use currying. Then we will analyze the program, and I will show you another version of it that uses the concept of currying.

Program Without Currying

In the upcoming program, there is a function that accepts two arguments. When you invoke the function, you pass all the required arguments. Otherwise, you cannot proceed. OOP developers are already familiar with this kind of coding. As mentioned, the concept of currying is not used in this program.

Demonstration 1

Here is the complete program that does not use currying:

```
using static System.Console;
WriteLine("Analyzing a non-curried function.");
int a = 10, b = 2;
int result = new Sample().AddTwoNumbers(a,b);
WriteLine($"{a}+{b} is {result}");

class Sample
{
    public Func<int, int, int> AddTwoNumbers =
        (int first, int second) => first + second;
}
```

Output

This program is straightforward; it produces the following output:

```
Analyzing a non-curried function.
10+2 is 12
```

Analysis

As mentioned, passing the required number of arguments was mandatory to invoke the AddTwoNumbers function in this program. For example, if you do not supply two integer arguments and use the following code:

```
int result = new Sample().AddTwoNumbers(a);
```

you will receive the following compile-time error:

```
Error CS7036 There is no argument given that corresponds to the required
formal parameter 'arg2' of 'Func<int, int, int>'
```

Now the question is, what is the problem with this approach? The answer is obvious: both arguments should be ready (or, available) before you invoke the function. This is where currying can help you. Let's see the next program.

Using the Concept of Currying

The following program is an alternative version of the previous program. This time I use the concept of currying. In this program, I used an extension method called Curry, which is defined in the following namespace as follows:

```
namespace CustomLibrary
{
    public static class CurryExtensions
    {
        public static Func<int, Func<int, int>> Curry(this
          Func<int, int, int> f)
          {
              return x => y => f(x, y);
          }
    }
}
```

POINT TO NOTE

I probably do not need to remind you that you can use the expression body syntax as well. For example, the Curry function can be defined as follows:

```
public static Func<int, Func<int, int>> Curry (this Func<int, int, int> f) =>
    x => y => f(x, y);
```

So, if you want, you can follow a similar style of coding. In this book, I have shown you both approaches.

The introduction of this extension method allows me to use two more approaches to invoke the AddTwoNumbers function.

New approach 1:

```
int total = new Sample().AddTwoNumbers.Curry()(a)(b);
WriteLine($"{a}+{b} is {total}");
```

New approach 2:

```
var afterFirstNumber = new Sample().AddTwoNumbers.Curry()(a);
int afterSecondNumber = afterFirstNumber(b);
WriteLine($"{a}+{b} is {afterSecondNumber}");
```

In each approach, I pass the function arguments a and b separately. Notice that in the first approach, you pass parameters separately inside brackets: (). But in the second approach, you invoke the function with one argument. Then the function waits for the second argument, which you pass next. Before we discuss the advantage of this approach, let's see the complete program with the corresponding output.

Note   You do not need to call the Curry() function repeatedly. Once it is executed, you can continue currying.

Demonstration 2

Here is the complete program. I have retained the comments to help you understand it. Notice the important changes in bold.

```csharp
using CustomLibrary;
using static System.Console;
WriteLine("Applying the concept of currying.");
int a = 10, b = 2;
// Common approach
int result = new Sample().AddTwoNumbers(a, b);
// var result1 = new Sample().AddTwoNumbers(a); // Error CS7036
WriteLine($"{a}+{b} is {result}");

// New approach-1
int total = new Sample().AddTwoNumbers.Curry()(a)(b);
WriteLine($"{a}+{b} is {total}");

// New approach-2
var afterFirstNumber = new Sample().AddTwoNumbers.Curry()(a);
int afterSecondNumber = afterFirstNumber(b);
WriteLine($"{a}+{b} is {afterSecondNumber}");

class Sample
{
    public Func<int, int, int> AddTwoNumbers =
      (int first, int second) => first + second;
}

namespace CustomLibrary
{
    public static class CurryExtensions
    {
        public static Func<int, Func<int, int>> Curry(this
          Func<int, int, int> f)
          {
            return x => y => f(x, y);
          }
    }
}
```

Output

Each of these approaches of invoking the AddTwoNumbers function produces identical output.

```
Analyzing a curried function.
10+2 is 12
10+2 is 12
10+2 is 12
```

Analysis

Note the following about the previous program:

- **You can extend this concept when you consider a greater number of arguments**. For example, if you have the following function inside the Sample class:

  ```
  public Func<int, int, int, int> AddThreeNumbers =
    (int x, int y, int z) => x + y + z;
  ```

  you can create a new extension method as follows:

  ```
  public static Func<int, Func<int, Func<int, int>>>
    Curry(this Func<int, int, int, int> f)
      {
        return x => y => z => f(x, y, z);
      }
  ```

  Then you can add three integers as follows:

  ```
  var after1stNumber = new Sample().AddThreeNumbers.Curry()(10);
  var after2ndNumber = after1stNumber(20);
  var after3rdNumber = after2ndNumber(30);
  WriteLine($"10+20+30 is {after3rdNumber}");
  ```

- **You can see that when you invoke a curried function, you do not need to pass all the arguments at the same time**. Instead, you can wait, do some meaningful operation, and continue the function execution.

- I used the implicit type `var` in the following statement:

  ```
  var afterFirstNumber = new Sample().AddTwoNumbers(a);
  ```

  You know that you can use the explicit type `Func<int, int>` instead of using the `var` keyword and replace the previous line of code with the following line:

  ```
  Func<int,int> afterFirstNumber= new Sample().AddTwoNumbers(a);
  ```

- You may note that you can pass the arguments separated by brackets too. The following code segment shows how this works:

  ```
  var finalResult = new Sample().AddThreeNumbers.Curry()(10)(20)(30);
  WriteLine($"10+20+30 is {finalResult}");
  ```

Q&A Session

5.1 I understand that I do not need to supply all the arguments to invoke a function using currying. But when you do not supply them, you delay the overall function execution time. Why should I accept this delay?

In certain applications, you may see a function that requires some special arguments that will be constructed based on other factors. So, you cannot call the function until those special arguments are ready. It is also possible that you wait for a third-party call to get some arguments. If you follow the traditional approach, you must wait. But as mentioned, currying helps you in such a scenario. Applying the currying technique, instead of waiting for all these arguments, you can invoke the function with the arguments that are available, and then you can wait for the remaining arguments to finish the function invocation call.

You may also note that if a function needs to have multiple parameters, you can hide the complexity of this function. For example, by applying the currying mechanism, you get a simplified function in which you can pass fewer parameters.

5.2 I believe that the use of generic methods in Demonstration 2 (or Demonstration 3) can provide more flexibility. Is this correct?

Yes, you are making good progress. Generics are advanced concepts. In my example, my extension method (Curry) is simple, so I did not complicate the code. But as I said, the use of generics can provide more flexibility because to add two noninteger numbers (such as 10.5 and 4.5), you cannot use the following Curry function:

```
public static Func<int, Func<int, int>> Curry(this
 Func<int, int, int> f)
  {
   return x => y => f(x, y);
  }
```

You cannot do this because these are floating-point numbers.

To overcome this, you can use the following method, which will work for both integers and nonintegers.

```
public static Func<T, Func<T, T>> GenericCurry<T>(this
 Func<T, T, T> f)
  {
    return x => y => f(x, y);
  }
```

In fact, I'll show you the use of the third-party library Curryfy shortly. This library includes lots of generic extension methods to help you apply the concept of currying.

5.3 You have shown that if a function has three parameters, I can pass one argument at a time by applying the concept of currying. But is there any way to vary the number of arguments? In other words, instead of passing one argument at a time, can I pass two arguments (separated by commas) in the first phase and the remaining argument in the next phase?

You are basically asking about the concept of partial application, which I did not discuss. The goal of this chapter was to analyze functional composition using currying. But if you understand Demonstration 2 and the corresponding analysis section, you can easily make such a program using the extension methods. To elaborate on this, I present the following program where I show you three possible case studies:

- **Case 1:** Passing arguments one by one in three different phases

- **Case 2:** Passing two arguments in the first phase and then one argument in the next phase

- **Case 3:** Passing one argument in the first phase and then two arguments in the next phase

Refer to the following program's comments for easy reference.

Demonstration 3

Here is the complete program:

```
using CustomLibrary;
using static System.Console;
WriteLine("Applying the concept of currying and partial
 application.");
int a = 10, b = 20, c = 30;
// Case-1: Adding the arguments one-by-one
var after1stNumber = new Sample().AddThreeNumbers.Curry()(a);
var after2ndNumber = after1stNumber(b);
var after3rdNumber = after2ndNumber(c);
WriteLine($"a+b+c is {after3rdNumber}");

// Case-2: Passing one argument, and then
// two arguments( separated by commas)
var afterA = new Sample().AddThreeNumbers.UsePartial()(a);
var afterBandC = afterA(b, c);
WriteLine($"a+b+c is {afterBandC}");

// Case-3: Passing two arguments,and then
// then one argument( separated by commas)
var afterAandB = new Sample().AddThreeNumbers.UsePartial2()(a, b);
var afterC = afterAandB(c);
WriteLine($"a+b+c is {afterC}");
```

```
class Sample
{
   public Func<int, int, int, int> AddThreeNumbers =
   (int x, int y, int z) => x + y + z;
}

namespace CustomLibrary
{
    public static class CurryExtensions
    {
        public static Func<int, Func<int, Func<int, int>>>
         Curry(this Func<int, int, int, int> f)
         {
            return x => y => z => f(x, y, z);
         }
        public static Func<int, Func<int, int, int>>
         UsePartial(this Func<int, int, int, int> f)
         {
            return x => (y, z) => x + y + z;
         }
        public static Func<int, int, Func<int, int>>
         UsePartial2(this Func<int, int, int, int> f)
         {
            return (x, y) => z => x + y + z;
         }
    }
}
```

Output

Here is the output of the program. The identical output of this program confirms you can choose the approach that suits your needs best.

```
Applying the concept of currying and partial application.
a+b+c is 60
a+b+c is 60
a+b+c is 60
```

Note   I'll also demonstrate currying using the Curryfy library shortly. It is an external library and includes built-in functions to make applications that support the concepts of currying and partial application. The current owner of the library is Leandro Vieira. I'd like to thank him, who reviewed several chapters in this book. I am also thankful to him for permitting me to use his library in this book. You can learn more about this library at `https://github.com/leandromoh/Curryfy`.

Currying is a functional programming technique. Demonstration 2 and Demonstration 3 discussed this technique for simple scenarios. Let's discuss a complex problem that can help you understand the importance of currying better. Before that, I'd like to talk about the use of external libraries.

Using External NuGet Packages

In this book, you have seen me using `System.Linq` and `System.Collections.Immutable`. They provide built-in support to write functional-style code. But you know that C# is primarily an object-oriented programming language. So, from the functional programmer's point of view, there is still a big gap that needs to be filled by providing support for specific functionalities. This is why many independent developers have written libraries.

As an example, consider Demonstration 3 where you saw me use three extension methods inside the `CustomLibrary` namespace. You understand that I needed those extension methods to apply the currying mechanism. Adding the functions in the `CustomLibrary` in the same way and showing their presence in a program where all of them are not required may not be a good idea. Instead, I could keep those functions in a separate library and call the library functions whenever I need them. This approach makes the code cleaner. Since the program was simple, I preferred to write only necessary functions instead of using a big library. If you do not have built-in support for a particular functionality, you have the following options:

- You can write the necessary functions and use them. If there are lots of functions, it'll be better to make a library that can contain these functions.

- Alternatively, you can use a third-party library that is easily available. So, you can install the required NuGet package in your project.

Using Curryfy

In the upcoming discussion, I'll use an external library called Curryfy. I have found that it is very useful when you apply currying. This library contains lots of other functionalities (such as support for partial application) too. To demonstrate currying, I can use the Curry() function from this library. At the same time, you will also get used to the idea of using an external library.

POINT TO NOTE

A NuGet package contains reusable code (aka libraries) that other developers have already developed. They share these libraries so that you can use them in your project. Microsoft provides (https://learn.microsoft.com/en-us/nuget/quickstart/install-and-use-a-package-in-visual-studio) step-by-step instructions on to install and use a NuGet package in Visual Studio for Windows. I have used NuGet Package Manager to install the Curryfy library in my system. There are alternative options too. You can use NuGet Package Manager, Package Manager Console, or .NET CLI to install the desired package.

If you want to know about the NuGet documentation, you can refer to https://learn.microsoft.com/en-us/nuget/. This page clearly states that NuGet client tools provide the ability to produce and consume the libraries as packages.

Q&A Session

5.4 My understanding is that using a third-party library can bring unnecessary dependencies to my project. Is this correct?

True. No one will restrict you from using a library that you build yourself. But using a third-party library can provide you with the following benefits:

- You save on development time. Instead of making everything from scratch, you can try the third-party code to verify a concept instantly.

- If the library is well-known and widely used, a community of developers continuously uses it and shares feedback. As a result, you get periodical bug fixes and automatic updates.

- By using a well-known third-party library, you'll probably end up with a better-designed and robust solution since its design is constantly revisited by the community.

Case Study

Before I demonstrate the next program, let's understand the essence of currying with a case study: there is a shopkeeper who sells different products. To attract customers, he provides different discounts before he calculates the final price of the product. Customers also know that they will get some discounts, but they do not know about the exact discounts. To clarify, let's assume the following points:

- Customers can buy various products. Each product has a maximum retail price (MRP) tag. (It is called as manufacturer's suggested retail price in certain countries.) I use the Product class for this purpose where each product is initialized with the MRP.

- To attract customers, the shopkeeper issues a seasonal discount on the MRP. This discount varies between 1 percent to 14 percent. This is the reason that you'll see the following code inside the Product class:

```
// Get a seasonal discount
int seasonalDiscount = new Random().Next(1,15);
```

- To attract more customers, the shopkeeper initiates some coupons to provide more discounts. But there is a trick that a customer does not know: if the seasonal discount is less than 10 percent, the shopkeeper provides an additional 5 percent discount. Otherwise, the seller gives the customer up to a 2 percent more discount on the MRP. This is the reason that you'll see the following code inside the Product class:

```
// Get a coupon discount
int couponDiscount =
seasonalDiscount < 10 ? 5 : new Random().Next(1, 3);
```

- After applying both types of discounts, the final price of the product is calculated as follows:

```
mrp - (mrp * seasonal / 100) - (mrp * coupon / 100);
```

- In the upcoming program, you'll see a lambda function to perform this calculation. It is as follows:

```
public Func<double, int, int, double> GetFinalCost =
  (mrp, seasonal, coupon) =>
    mrp - (mrp * seasonal / 100) - (mrp * coupon / 100);
```

- The most important point is that to calculate the final price, you need to know about the seasonal discount and the coupon discount. Also, in this example, you do not know the coupon discount until you know the seasonal discount. If you follow the imperative style of coding, you must wait to get these values before performing the final calculation to determine the product's price.

- You may think that the overall calculation is simple. But remember that it is an artificial example to demonstrate the use of currying. This calculation can be time-consuming if you rely on some external services to calculate these discounts and the response time from those external services is not immediate because of various factors. So, the overall calculation can be time-consuming because you cannot proceed until you know the discounts.

- Finally, I have placed the GetPriceAfterDiscount function in a separate class called IO. Though it was not required, I did this intentionally. Can you guess the reason? Yes, as you progress more on FP, you'll learn that separating impurities from pure functions is a better practice. You'll learn more about this topic in Chapter 6.

Let's now discuss the implementation.

Demonstration 4

In this situation, currying can help you. You can split the GetFinalCost function into a function that takes one input and produces one output. Using the Curry function from the Curryfy library, I can calculate the final price of a product as follows (notice the important steps in bold):

```
var mrp = GetFinalCost.Curry()(product.MRP);
// Get a seasonal discount( the calculations are not shown)
// Calculate cost after seasonal discount
var afterSeasonalDiscount = mrp(seasonalDiscount);
// Get a coupon discount( the calculations are not shown)
// Calculate cost after coupon discount
var afterCouponDiscount = afterSeasonalDiscount(couponDiscount);
```

You should be able to understand the remaining parts of the following program:

```
using Curryfy;
using static System.Console;
WriteLine("*** Using the concept of currying.***\n");
Product product1 = new(100);
double product1Price = IO.GetPriceAfterDiscount(product1);
WriteLine($"MRP: ${product1.MRP}, Final price:
 ${product1Price}\n");

Product product2 = new(200);
double product2Price = IO.GetPriceAfterDiscount(product2);
WriteLine($"MRP: ${product2.MRP}, Final price:
 ${product2Price}\n");

class Product
{
    public double MRP { get; }
    public Product(double mrp)
    {
        MRP = mrp;
    }
    // Price calculator after discounts
    public Func<double, int, int, double> GetFinalCost =
    (mrp, seasonal,coupon) =>
      mrp - (mrp * seasonal / 100)- (mrp * coupon / 100);

}
```

```
class IO
{
    public static double GetPriceAfterDiscount(Product product)
    {
        var mrp = product.GetFinalCost.Curry()(product.MRP);
        // Get a seasonal discount
        int seasonalDiscount = new Random().Next(1, 15);
        // Calculate cost after seasonal discount
        WriteLine($"Seasonal Discount={seasonalDiscount}%");
        var afterSeasonalDiscount = mrp(seasonalDiscount);

        // Get a coupon discount
        int couponDiscount =
         seasonalDiscount < 10 ? 5 : new Random().Next(1, 3);
        // Calculate cost after coupon discount
        WriteLine($"Coupon discount={couponDiscount}%");
        var afterCouponDiscount = afterSeasonalDiscount(couponDiscount);
        return afterCouponDiscount;
    }

}
```

Output

Here is sample output from this program:

```
*** Using the concept of currying.***
Seasonal Discount=11%
Coupon discount=1%
MRP: $100, Final price: $88

Seasonal Discount=4%
Coupon discount=5%
MRP: $200, Final price: $182
```

You know that random values can be different in your system. So, here is some more sample output that shows the different discount amounts for identical purchases:

```
*** Using the concept of currying.***
Seasonal Discount=1%
Coupon discount=5%
MRP: $100, Final price: $94

Seasonal Discount=10%
Coupon discount=2%
MRP: $200, Final price: $176
```

Analysis

You can relate to this scenario when you see holiday sales in certain shops. This program gives you a feel of a lottery system too.

Q&A Session

5.5 Can you summarize the benefits of currying?

Q&A 5.1 already described that by applying currying, instead of waiting for all the function arguments, you can process the partial invocation of the function with the arguments that are already available. Then you wait for other arguments to complete the function call. Since partial function processing can be done in advance, you can speed up the overall performance of your application.

You'll also notice that if you keep applying currying, in each step, the signatures of the functions get simpler (you can also refer to the solution of E5.1 in this context). So, if you need to process a complex function, you can make the computation easy by applying currying.

In addition, using the currying concept, you can create and use a partial application on the fly.

Lastly, when you process the partial invocation, you get back a delegate. In Chapter 1, you have seen that delegates in C# represent functions and functions are first-class citizens in C#, so you get the corresponding benefits. For example, you can pass them to another higher-order function.

Exercises

E5.1 Consider three simple integers 2, 5, and 7. Can you write a simple program to calculate the sum of these numbers using currying?

E5.2 Predict the output of the following program:

```
using static System.Console;
WriteLine("Exercise 5.2");
Func<int, Func<int, string>> compare =
 x => y => (x > y ? $"{x} is greater"
                  : $"{y} is greater");
string result=compare(23)(12);
WriteLine(result);
result = compare(23)(37);
WriteLine(result);
```

E5.3 Demonstration 4 uses the Curryfy library. Can you rewrite the function without using this library?

E5.4 Some code in the following program is missing.

```
using CustomLibrary;
using static System.Console;

var add10 = new Sample().AddNumbers(10);
var add20 = add10(20);
WriteLine($"10+20 is:{add20}");

// Uncurrying
var uncurried = new Sample().AddNumbers.UnCurry();
var result = uncurried(25, 35);
WriteLine($"25+35 is:{result}");

class Sample
{
  public Func<int, Func<int, int>> AddNumbers = x => y => x + y;
}
```

// Some code is missing here

When you run this program, it shows the following output:

```
10+20 is:30
25+35 is:60
```

Can you write the missing part?

E5.5 Can you compile the following code? If so, can you predict the output?

```
using CustomLibrary;
using static System.Console;
WriteLine("Exercise 5.5");
int a = 10, b = 20, c = 30;

var afterA = new Sample().Calculate.UsePartial()(a);
var afterBandC = afterA(b, c);

WriteLine($"{b} * {c} + {a} is {afterBandC}");

class Sample
{
    public Func<int, int, int, int> Calculate =
      (int x, int y, int z) => y * z + x;
}

namespace CustomLibrary
{
    public static class Extensions
    {
        public static Func<int, Func<int, int, int>>
          UsePartial(this Func<int, int, int, int> f)
        {
            return x => (y, z) => f(x,y,z);
        }
    }
}
```

E5.6 Can you compile the following code? If so, can you predict the output?

```
using CustomLibrary;
using static System.Console;
WriteLine("Exercise 5.6");

var afterTwoInputs = new Sample().Display.UsePartial()("red", "green");
var afterLastInput = afterTwoInputs("yellow");
WriteLine($"{afterLastInput}");
class Sample
{
    public Func<string, string, string, string> Display =
     (string x, string y, string z) => $"{x},{y},{z}";
}

namespace CustomLibrary
{
    public static class Extensions
    {
        public static Func<string, string, Func<string, string>>
         UsePartial(this Func<string, string, string, string> f)
        {
            return (x, y) => z => $"Mixing {z} with {y} and {x}.";
        }
    }
}
```

Summary

This chapter gave you an overview of functional composition using currying. It answered the following questions:

- What is currying?

- How can you benefit from the currying technique?

- How can you make a curried function from a noncurried function (and vice versa)?

- How does the NuGet package help you?

- How can you use the curry function from the Curryfy library in your project?

Solutions to Exercises

Here are the solutions.

E5.1

```
using static System.Console;
WriteLine("Exercise 5.1");
Func<int, Func<int, Func<int, int>>> sum =
 x => y => z => x + y + z;
Func<int, Func<int, int>> temp1 = sum(2);
Func<int, int> temp2 = temp1(5);
int result = temp2(7);
WriteLine($"2+5+7={result}");
```

This program produces the following output:

```
Exercise 5.1
2+5+7=14
```

Author's note I have intentionally used explicit declarations instead of using the var keyword in the corresponding lines to demonstrate that in each step, the function signatures of the functions get simpler as you apply currying.

E5.2

This program produces the following output:

```
Exercise 5.2
23 is greater
37 is greater
```

E5.3

Notice that the GetPriceAfterDiscount() function in Demonstration 4 uses the Curry() function from the Curryfy library. It is the only place where you use the Curryfy library. If you do not want to use an external library, you can write custom extension methods to achieve the same task. I have included both the generic and nongeneric versions for currying. You can use any of them. The following program uses the generic version for currying (the comments are for your reference):

```
using CustomLibrary;
using static System.Console;
WriteLine("*** Using the concept of currying.***");
Product product1 = new(100);
double product1Price = IO.GetPriceAfterDiscount(product1);
WriteLine($"MRP: ${product1.MRP}, Final price: ${product1Price}\n");

Product product2 = new(200);
double product2Price = IO.GetPriceAfterDiscount(product2);
WriteLine($"MRP: ${product2.MRP}, Final price: ${product2Price}\n");

class Product
{
    public double MRP { get; }
    public Product(double mrp)
    {
        MRP = mrp;
    }
    // Price calculator after discounts
    public Func<double, int, int, double> GetFinalCost =
      (mrp, seasonal, coupon) =>
        mrp - (mrp * seasonal / 100) - (mrp * coupon / 100);
}
class IO
{
    // The following function does not use the Curryfy library
    public static double GetPriceAfterDiscount(Product product)
    {
```

```csharp
        // Using a non-generic version
        // var mrp = product
        //              .GetFinalCost
        //              .NonGenericCurry()(product.MRP);
        // Using the generic version
        var mrp = product
                    .GetFinalCost
                    .GenericCurry()(product.MRP);
        // Get a seasonal discount
        int seasonalDiscount = new Random().Next(1, 15);
        // Calculate cost after seasonal discount
        WriteLine($"Seasonal Discount={seasonalDiscount}%");
        var afterSeasonalDiscount = mrp(seasonalDiscount);

        // Get a coupon discount
        int couponDiscount = seasonalDiscount < 10
                                ? 5 : new Random().Next(1, 3);
        // Calculate cost after coupon discount
        WriteLine($"Coupon discount={couponDiscount}%");
        var afterCouponDiscount = afterSeasonalDiscount(couponDiscount);
        return afterCouponDiscount;
    }
}

namespace CustomLibrary
{
    public static class CurryExtensions
    {
        public static Func<double, Func<int, Func<int,
         double>>> NonGenericCurry(
          this Func<double, int, int, double> f)
        {
            return x => y => z => f(x, y, z);
        }
```

```
    public static Func<T1, Func<T2, Func<T3, TResult>>>
     GenericCurry<T1, T2, T3, TResult>
      (this Func<T1, T2, T3, TResult> f)
    {
        return (T1 x) => (T2 y) => (T3 z) => f(x, y, z);
    }
  }
}
```

E5.4

This program uses the concept of uncurrying. Here is the complete program with the key segment in bold:

```
using CustomLibrary;
using static System.Console;

var add10 = new Sample().AddNumbers(10);
var add20 = add10(20);
WriteLine($"10+20 is:{add20}");

// using extension method
var uncurried = new Sample().AddNumbers.UnCurry();
var result = uncurried(25, 35);
WriteLine($"25+35 is:{result}");

class Sample
{
 public Func<int, Func<int, int>> AddNumbers =
  x => y => x + y;
}

namespace CustomLibrary
{
    public static class CurryExtensions
    {
        public static Func<int, int, int> UnCurry(this
         Func<int, Func<int, int>> f)
```

```
    {
        return (int x, int y) => f(x)(y);
    }
  }
}
```

When you download the source code from the Apress website, you'll see the generic version of UnCurry too.

E5.5

Yes. This program produces the following output:

```
Exercise 5.5
20 * 30 + 10 is 610
```

E5.6

Yes. This program produces the following output:

```
Exercise 5.6
Mixing yellow with green and red.
```

CHAPTER 6

Handling Temporal Coupling

Cohesion and coupling are two important concepts in software engineering. Wikipedia (`https://en.wikipedia.org/wiki/Cohesion_(computer_science)`) states the following:

> *The software metrics of coupling and cohesion were invented by Larry Constantine in the late 1960s as part of Structured Design, based on characteristics of "good" programming practices that reduced maintenance and modification costs.*

What is cohesion? The dictionary definition of *cohesion* is "interconnection" or "unity." In simple terms, it is a degree of measure to which we unite particular module elements to serve a well-defined purpose. The other one is *coupling*, which measures the degree of interdependence between software modules. While coding, developers aim for high cohesion and low coupling. This is standard practice for component-level design.

There are several categories of cohesion and coupling. If interested, you can learn more about them from any software engineering book. Our aim is not to dig into these concepts in this chapter. Instead, we will discuss a common type of coupling, called *temporal coupling*, that is often seen in day-to-day programming. This kind of coupling is often necessary, but if you do not handle it properly, you'll get unwanted results. The unwanted effects of this kind of coupling can be removed (or loosened) using the concept of immutability that you learned in Chapter 3. This chapter discusses the approach. In addition, at the end of the chapter, you will find a nice strategy to separate the I/O from the core functions. This kind of separation is useful to reduce dependencies and side effects in the code.

© Vaskaran Sarcar 2023
V. Sarcar, *Introducing Functional Programming Using C#*, https://doi.org/10.1007/978-1-4842-9697-4_6

Temporal Coupling Overview

Often we see programs where you invoke multiple functions in a particular order but there is no hint about the correct order sequence. As a result, the code depends on human interpretations and becomes prone to errors.

How Does This Happen?

Let's assume there are three activities: A, B, and C. You need to complete Activity A before you start Activity B, and you can start Activity C only after the completion of Activity B. If you represent these activities using functions, you can say that you invoke the functions in sequential order (first A, then B, and finally C). Assume that you use some shared states, and these functions update those states. This approach causes the problem. Demonstration 1 will make it clearer to you.

Later, you'll understand that without the shared state, the temporal coupling cannot occur. So, to remove (or reduce) the effect of temporal coupling, you can refactor the code by deleting the shared states and promoting immutability. Demonstration 2 will show you the approach.

Q&A Session

6.1 You are suggesting I delete the shared states. At the same time, you are saying that you promote immutability. Can you elaborate on this?

When you delete the shared states, how can you pass the data? You pass the data in function arguments and return values. In other words, you make things immutable. As I said before, Demonstration 2 will make this clearer to you.

Recognizing the Problem

Before you cure a disease, you must identify it. So, recognizing the temporal coupling along with its effects in a program is important before you remove it from your code or reduce its unwanted effects. This is the reason I'll start with a simple program that runs successfully but suffers from temporal coupling.

A Program That Suffers from Temporal Coupling

This program shows the construction of licensed vehicles. Let's assume that the overall process is divided into three different parts, as follows:

- Installing an engine

- Completing the remaining parts of the vehicle

- Adding a license

You will see four participating classes in this program: Engine, Vehicle, VehicleMaker, and Output. Our focus will be on the VehicleMaker class that contains some useful functions: InstallEngine, CompleteBody, AddLicense, Display, and Validate. Before you see the complete program, note the following:

- First, get the engine ready. Before you start working on the vehicle body, you check whether the engine is installed. See the following code:

```
void CompleteBody(BodyType bodyType)
{
 // Install the engine before working on the vehicle body.
 _engine.Install();
 _vehicle = new Vehicle(bodyType, _engine);
}
```

- Once the vehicle's construction process is done, you can add a license to it. See the following function:

```
void AddLicense()
{
  _vehicle.AddLicence();
}
```

- Now you understand that you start manufacturing a vehicle by installing an engine. Then, you complete the remaining parts of the body. Finally, you add a license. This is why you'll use the following function to validate a vehicle instance:

```
    public void Validate(EngineType engineType, BodyTypeg bodyType)
    {
    // The following calling sequence is OK
     InstallEngine(engineType);
     CompleteBody(bodyType);
     AddLicense();
     Display(_vehicle);
     // Some other code, if any
    }
```

- There are two enum types, called EngineType and BodyType. These are used to set an engine type and vehicle body, respectively.

Note   To make the program simple and focus on the key topics, I do not employ any kind of input validations.

The remaining parts are easy. You should be able to understand the following program now.

Demonstration 1

Here is the complete program:

```
using static System.Console;
WriteLine("***Experimenting Temporal Coupling.***");
VehicleMaker maker = new();
maker.Validate(EngineType.Electric, BodyType.Sports);
enum EngineType
{
    Electric,
    InternalCombustion,
    Hybrid
}
```

```
enum BodyType
{
    Sports,
    Standard
}
class Engine
{
    private EngineType Type { get; }
    public string Status { get; set; }
    public Engine(
      EngineType engineType,
      string engineStatus = "not set")
    {
        Type = engineType;
        Status = engineStatus;
    }
    public void Install()
    {
        Status = "installed";

    }
    public override string ToString()
    {
        return $"{Type} engine is {Status}";
    }
}

class Vehicle
{
    private BodyType Body { get; }
    private Engine Engine { get; }
    public bool LicenseStatus { get; set; }
    public Vehicle(
      BodyType body,
```

```
    Engine engine,
    bool licenseStatus = false)
{
    Body = body;
    Engine = engine;
    LicenseStatus = licenseStatus;
}
public void AddLicence()
{
    LicenseStatus = true;
}

public override string ToString()
{
    return $"""
            The vehicle's description:
            Engine: {Engine}
            Body: {Body}
            License status: {LicenseStatus}
            """;
}
}

class VehicleMaker
{
    private Engine _engine;
    private Vehicle _vehicle;
    void InstallEngine(EngineType engineType)
    {
        _engine = new Engine(engineType);
    }
    void CompleteBody(BodyType bodyType)
    {
        // Install the engine before working on the
        // vehicle body.
```

```
        engine.Install();              _
        _vehicle = new Vehicle(bodyType, _engine);
    }
    void AddLicense()
    {
        vehicle.AddLicence();          _
    }
    void Display(Vehicle vehicle)
    {
        Output.ShowStatus(vehicle);
    }

    public void Validate(EngineType engineType, BodyType bodyType)
    {
        // The following calling sequence is OK
        InstallEngine(engineType);
        CompleteBody(bodyType);
        AddLicense();
        Display(_vehicle);
        //Some other code, if any
    }
}
class Output
{
    public static void ShowStatus(Vehicle vehicle)
    {
        WriteLine(vehicle);
    }
}
```

Output

Once you run this program, you will see the following output:

```
***Experimenting Temporal Coupling.***
The vehicle's description:
Engine: Electric engine is installed
Body: Sports
The license status: True
```

How Does It Cause Problems?

Let's take a close look at the following function:

```
public void Validate(EngineType engineType, BodyType bodyType)
{
    // The following calling sequence is OK
    InstallEngine(engineType);
    CompleteBody(bodyType);
    AddLicense();
    Display(_vehicle);
    // Some other code, if any
}
```

You can see that invoking the Validate function invokes the following three functions sequentially: InstallEngine, CompleteBody, and AddLicense. As per our initial assumptions, you should not change the calling sequence. **Interestingly, if you reorder them, your code can compile, but you will see erroneous output.** For example, the following calling sequences will compile successfully, but you will see the System.NullReferenceException:

```
// The following calling sequence causes the run-time error
CompleteBody(bodyType);
InstallEngine(engineType);
AddLicense();
```

Figure 6-1 shows that a runtime exception occurred because of the presence of temporal coupling in the program (note that _engine was null).

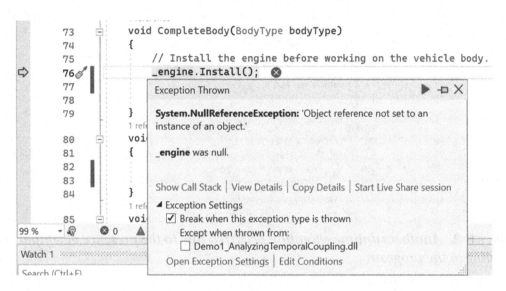

Figure 6-1. *A runtime exception occurred due to the presence of temporal coupling in the program*

Similarly, though the following calling sequences will compile, they will cause the runtime exception too:

```
// The following calling sequence also causes the run-time error
AddLicense();
CompleteBody(bodyType);
InstallEngine(engineType);
```

Figure 6-2 shows another runtime exception that occurs because of the presence of temporal coupling in the program (note that _vehicle was null).

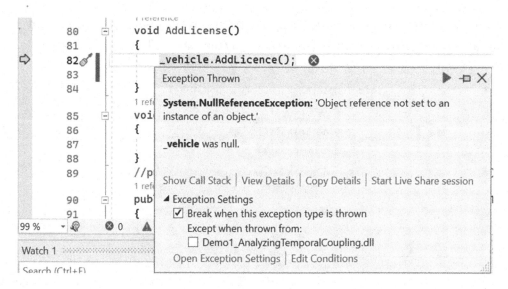

Figure 6-2. *Another runtime exception occurred due to the presence of temporal coupling in the program*

Q&A Session

6.2 By seeing the previous exceptions, it appears to me that you could block these exceptions by introducing null checks. For example, if I replace the lines `_engine.InstallEngine();` and `_vehicle.CheckVehicleStatus();` with `_engine?. InstallEngine();` and `_vehicle?.CheckVehicleStatus();`, respectively, I will not see any runtime exception. Am I correct?

It is true that if you use these proposed lines, you will not see the runtime exceptions, but you should remember that blocking the NullReferenceException is not the only goal here. In fact, we do not want to work with a null vehicle or a null engine, and we'd like to see the error when it appears. The real purpose of using these methods is to demonstrate that the *incorrect calling sequence causes unwanted state to be passed downstream for further processing.* For example, with your proposed solution, the calling sequence

```
CompleteBody(bodyType);
InstallEngine(engineType);
AddLicense();
Display(_vehicle);
```

will produce the following output now:

```
***Experimenting Temporal Coupling.***
The vehicle's description:
Engine:
Body: Sports
The license status: True
```

Can you see the null engine? Similarly, the following calling sequence is problematic too:

```
AddLicense();
CompleteBody(bodyType);
InstallEngine(engineType);
Display(_vehicle);
```

It will produce the following output now:

```
***Experimenting Temporal Coupling.***
The vehicle's description:
Engine:
Body: Sports
The license status: False
```

Can you see the vehicle without the license and the null engine?

From each of these output segments, you know that there is something wrong with the code.

Removing the Effect

Compile-time errors can be your friends because you can take the necessary steps immediately to correct the program. On the contrary, runtime errors are evil! They cause the premature termination of a running program and surprise us. In fact, the runtime exceptions are one of the worst things that you want to see. This is why catching an error early is always a better idea. If you can rewrite this program to prevent the runtime error, you will improve the code quality. Now the question is, what is the first step?

You can see that the InstallEngine and CompleteBody functions caused side effects: they changed the states of the VehicleMaker instance. This was possible because the states were shared between these functions. Now you get a clue that without the shared states, the temporal coupling could not occur. Can you make a better program? Yes, you can. Continue reading.

A Better Program

As a first step toward making a better program, let's remove these states from the VehicleMaker class. In addition, to promote immutability further, I am about to use record class and with expression in the upcoming program. You saw them in Chapter 3. But you may note that VehicleMaker and Output classes do not hold any states in the upcoming program. This is why I do not make them the record type.

Also, in the refactored version, I do not need the Install() method inside the Engine class, so I removed the Status property from the Engine class too.

Demonstration 2

Here is the refactored version with the important changes in bold:

```
using static System.Console;
WriteLine("***Refactored version of demonstration 1.***");
VehicleMaker maker = new();
maker.Validate(EngineType.Electric, BodyType.Sports);
enum EngineType
{
    Electric,
    InternalCombustion,
    Hybrid
}
enum BodyType
{
    Sports,
    Standard
}
```

```
record class Engine
{
    private EngineType Type { get; }
    public Engine(EngineType engineType)
    {
        Type = engineType;
    }

    public override string ToString()
    {
        return $"{Type} engine is installed";
    }
}
record class Vehicle
{
    private BodyType Body { get; }
    private Engine Engine { get; }
    public bool LicenseStatus { get; set; }

    public Vehicle(
     BodyType body,
     Engine engine,
     bool licenseStatus = false)
    {
        Body = body;
        Engine = engine;
        LicenseStatus = licenseStatus;
    }
    public void AddLicence()
    {
        LicenseStatus = true;
    }
```

```csharp
    public override string ToString()
    {
        return $"""
                The vehicle's description:
                Engine: {Engine}
                Body: {Body}
                The license status: {LicenseStatus}
                """;
    }
}

class VehicleMaker
{
    Engine InstallEngine(EngineType engineType)
    {
        return new Engine(engineType);
    }
    Vehicle CompleteBody(BodyType bodyType, Engine engine)
    {
        return new Vehicle(bodyType, engine);
    }
    Vehicle AddLicense(Vehicle vehicle)
    {
        return vehicle with { LicenseStatus = true };
    }
    void Display(Vehicle vehicle)
    {
        Output.ShowStatus(vehicle);
    }
    public void Validate(EngineType engineType, BodyType bodyType)
    {
        // The following calling sequence is OK
        Engine engine = InstallEngine(engineType);
        Vehicle vehicle = CompleteBody(bodyType, engine);
```

```
        vehicle = AddLicense(vehicle);
        Display(vehicle);
        // Some other code, if any
    }
}
class Output
{
    public static void ShowStatus(Vehicle vehicle)
    {
        WriteLine(vehicle);
    }
}
```

Output

This program produces the same output except for the first line, which indicates that I have refactored the code.

```
***Refactored version of demonstration 1.***
The vehicle's description:
Engine: Electric engine is installed
Body: Sports
The license status: True
```

Analysis

Notice that this time if you reorder the calling sequence in the following code segment:

```
//  The following calling sequence causes compile-time error
Vehicle vehicle = CompleteBody(bodyType, engine);
Engine engine = InstallEngine(engineType);
vehicle = AddLicense(vehicle);
```

you will receive the compile-time error saying this:

```
Error CS0841 Cannot use local variable 'engine' before it is declared
```

Similarly, the following sequence will not compile too:

```
// The following calling sequence causes compile-time errors too
vehicle = AddLicense(vehicle);
Vehicle vehicle = CompleteBody(bodyType, engine);
Engine engine = InstallEngine(engineType);
```

In fact, the previous segment will cause two compile-time errors saying the following:

```
Error CS0165 Use of unassigned local variable 'vehicle'
Error CS0841 Cannot use local variable 'engine' before it is declared
```

Conclusion

You have exposed the temporal coupling by creating a chain of functions where each function produces the result for the next function. Now no one can call them out of order. Well done! We have removed the unwanted effects of the temporal coupling from the code!

POINT TO NOTE

In Demonstration 1, CompleteBody works on the Engine instance (_engine) and the Vehicle instance (_vehicle). But the method signature does not reflect this fact. Similarly, InstallEngine works on the Engine instance (_engine), but from the method signature you do not know this. (Here you pass a EngineType argument. I name the parameter engineType to give you only a hint that I am going to set an engine type.) So, these functions are dishonest.

But in Demonstration 2, CompleteBody and InstallEngine are honest functions. Functional programmers like to use honest functions because an honest function always honors its signature. So, the developers do not need to remember the hidden relationships among different parts of an application.

Q&A Session

6.3 Demonstration 2 gives me the idea that I will not see temporal coupling if there is no shared state. Is this correct?

Nice observation. Without the shared states, temporal coupling cannot occur. This is the reason I started the refactored version by deleting those shared states.

6.4 In Demonstration 1, the `Validate` function has the following definition:

```
public void Validate(EngineType engineType, BodyType bodyType)
{
    // The following calling sequence is OK
    InstallEngine(engineType);
    CompleteBody(bodyType);
    AddLicense();
    // Some other code, if any
}
```

In Demonstration 2, this function is restructured as follows:

```
public void Validate(EngineType engineType, BodyType bodyType)
{
    // The following calling sequence is OK
    Engine engine = InstallEngine(engineType);
    Vehicle vehicle = CompleteBody(bodyType, engine);
    vehicle = AddLicense(vehicle);
    // Some other code, if any
}
```

It appears to me that the `Validate` function in Demonstration 1 was cleaner compared to Demonstration 2. Am I correct?

Yes. But you have seen that it was hiding the relationships of the methods, and you have seen the associated problems. On the contrary, the refactored version does not suffer from temporal coupling, and it reflects the workflow clearly. In Demonstration 2, no one can mess up the calling sequence of these functions. Otherwise, the compiler will point out the error immediately.

6.5 You have talked about the honest functions. I'd like to hear more about them.

As mentioned, an honest function always honors its signature. For example, consider the following functions:

```
public static int Sum(int x, int y) => x + y;
public static string MakeDoubleAndConvert(int x)
{
    // Some other code skipped
    return (x * 2).ToString();
}
```

The Sum function says, give me two int arguments, and then I'll return an int. Similarly, the MakeDoubleAndConvert function says give me an int, and I'll return a string. These functions always do whatever they say. In other words, these functions behave like mathematical functions.

On the contrary, see the following function:

```
public static int DivideBy(int x,int y)=> x / y;
```

This function says, give me two int arguments, and I'll return an int. But it does not obey the contract always. You know that if y is 0, you will encounter the System.DivideByZeroException.

6.6 My understanding is that any function can fail due to various reasons, such as being out of memory or the hardware malfunctioning. In those cases, no function is honest at all. Is this correct?

In Chapter 1, while discussing purity and side effects, I told you the following:

> "We make assumptions about purity to some extent. This is because any function can fail due to some factors that are beyond our control. Consider the case of the "out of memory" error when your code did not cause the error, but it came from someone else's code which was executing in a parallel environment. Or, consider the case when the operating system (OS) itself crashes. If you consider cases like this, no function is 100% pure and this is the sad truth!"

The same comment applies to honest functions too. You can predict the behavior of an honest function by looking at its signature; they cannot surprise you by throwing an exception or a null value.

> **Note**   In Chapter 8, you'll see me using the `Either` type to handle two possible
> outcomes. I used this type for handling exceptions. At this stage, we do not need to
> complicate the discussion by considering the `Either` type.

6.7 I can see that in Demonstration 1, the following function exists:

```
void Display(Vehicle vehicle)
{
   Output.ShowStatus(vehicle);
}
```

You kept this function in Demonstration 2 also. Is it OK?

Yes. I have used this method to print the vehicle status in the console window. Since this
function does not cause any harm to our program apart from producing a side effect at
the end of the workflow, we can tolerate its presence in this program. In fact, let me tell
you this is a desirable side effect. It is not always possible to remove all the side effects
or state mutations in a program, particularly when you analyze the output. But we can
handle it in a better way. This is the reason you can see that I pushed the side effect to
the edge of the application but kept the core functions immutable.

**6.8 You said, "I pushed the side effect to the edge of the application but kept the core
functions immutable." Can you please elaborate?**

There is a pattern called Functional Core, Imperative Shell. It suggests separating the
business logic from the I/O. You can achieve this by writing the following:

- The business logic (core) following the functional style of
  programming

- The shell following the imperative style of programming.

Since the shell handles the outside world, you can use imperative programming
for those parts to allow state mutations and side effects. You may think of the design as
shown in Figure 6-3.

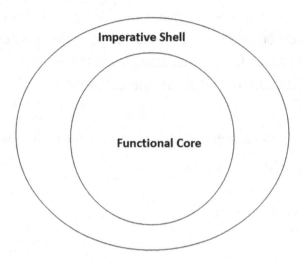

Figure 6-3. *Functional Core, Imperative Shell pattern*

Another important characteristic of this pattern is that you allow the shell to communicate with the core, but you do not allow the opposite. Following the dependency rule, the shell (outer circle) cannot impact the core (inner circle).

I like this pattern and used it in Demonstration 2.

Note   There are some nice articles written on the Functional Core, Imperative Shell pattern. Though they are not specific to C#, you will benefit from reading them. One such article can be found at `https://kennethlange.com/ functional-core-imperative-shell/#:~:text=The%20key%20 objectives%20in%20the,put%20it%20in%20the%20core`. If interested, you can also learn about the dependency rule from Robert C. Martin's famous book *Clean Architecture* (ISBN 978-0134494166).

This is the end of this chapter. The next chapter discusses the functional patterns and is quite big. Before you read that chapter, I hope you enjoyed this short chapter.

Exercises

E6.1 In this chapter, you learned about honest functions. Previously, you learned about pure functions. Can you distinguish between them?

E6.2 Can you relate temporal coupling with some real-world scenarios?

E6.3 In E6.4, you'll see a function as follows:

```
public void Execute()
{
  Initiate();
  ExecutePartOne();
  ExecutePartTwo();
  PrintStatus();
}
```

What is your opinion about this function design? Do you consider this a good design?

E6.4 There is a complex job that can be divided into two parts: part 1 and part 2. One can start executing part 2 if part 1 is already completed. To program this, assume that someone has written the following code:

```
using static System.Console;

new JobService().Execute();

class ComplexJob
{
    public bool partOneFinished, partTwoFinished;
    public ComplexJob(
      bool partOne = false,
      bool partTwo = false)
    {
        partOneFinished = partOne;
        partTwoFinished = partTwo;
    }

}
```

```
class JobService
{
    ComplexJob? _job;
    void Initiate()
    {
        _job = new ComplexJob();
    }
    void ExecutePartOne()
    {
        // Some code to finish Part 1
        _job.partOneFinished = true;
    }
    void ExecutePartTwo()
    {
        // Part 2 can be executed only after Part 1.
        // Some code to finish part 2
        _job.partTwoFinished = _job.partOneFinished;
    }
    void PrintStatus()
     {
       string Status = _job.partOneFinished &&
         _job.partTwoFinished
        ? "The process is completed successfully."
        : "Process is incomplete.";

       WriteLine(Status);
    }
    public void Execute()
    {
        Initiate();
        ExecutePartOne();
        ExecutePartTwo();
        PrintStatus();
    }
}
```

Can you find the improvement areas and predict the output?

E6.5 True or false? As developers, we should aim for high cohesion and low coupling.

Summary

As developers, we like to write code that does not suffer from coupling. Coupling can be of various forms, and one of them is temporal coupling. This type of coupling is not always easy to find and often unavoidable. But, immutability helps you remove the unwanted effects of temporal coupling from your code. This chapter explains the concept with examples. In brief, it covered the following topics:

- How can you detect temporal coupling in a program?

- What are the problems associated with temporal coupling?

- How does immutability help you remove the unwanted effects that come from the temporal coupling?

- How does the code reliability improve in the absence of temporal coupling?

- How can you separate the I/O using the Functional Core, Imperative Shell pattern?

Solutions to Exercises

Here are the solutions for the exercises in this chapter.

E6.1

If you compare the concepts of pure functions and honest functions, you can easily identify that pure functions are stricter than honest functions. In the case of honest functions, no one talks about side effects. The criterion for an honest function is simple: it should honor its signature so that you can have an idea about the possible output in advance.

Enrico Buonanno in his excellent book *Functional Programming in C#* (ISBN 9781617293955) summarizes the difference by saying the requirements for honest functions are less stringent compared to pure functions. He also pointed out the fact that though "honesty" is an informal term that is less technical and less stringent than purity, they are still useful.

E6.2

You can relate the scenario to the following real-world examples:

- Unless a student passes the final examination of class V, they cannot be promoted to class VI. And unless the student passes the final examination of class VI, the student cannot be promoted to class VII, and so on.

- Another example can be observed in holiday discounts where a seller provides some discount based on the purchase value. For example, if your purchase value is more than $2,000, the seller may decide to give you a 15 percent discount; otherwise, he gives you a 10 percent discount. You understand that in this example, the discount amount is calculated only after you complete the buying process.

- You must collect the ingredients and mix them properly with other materials to prepare a tasty dish. Notice that you cannot change the order of these activities; they are sequential.

E6.3

This looks clean, but it cannot be considered a good design if you hide the actual workflow (or, temporal coupling). This is because in such cases you suppress the relationships among these methods using some shared states. In other words, you do not prevent other developers who can alter this workflow and produce unwanted outcomes by executing the application.

E6.4

This program produces the following output:

```
The process is completed successfully.
```

This is an expected output, but if you saw Demonstration 2 and analyzed the problems of Demonstration 1, you can find the problem easily. For example, let's take a close look at the following function:

```
public void Execute()
{
    Initiate();
    ExecutePartOne();
    ExecutePartTwo();
    PrintStatus();
}
```

You can see that invoking the Execute function invokes the following four functions sequentially: Initiate, ExecutePartOne, ExecutePartTwo, and PrintStatus. **Interestingly, if you reorder them, your code can compile, but you will see a different output.** For example, the following calling sequences

```
ExecutePartOne();
Initiate();
ExecutePartTwo();
PrintStatus();
```

will cause a runtime exception, as shown in Figure 6-4.

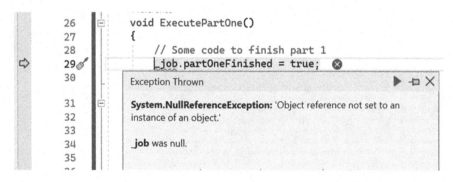

Figure 6-4. *A runtime exception occurred when you alter the calling sequence inside the Execute function*

The following calling sequence also causes a runtime exception:

```
PrintStatus();
ExecutePartOne();
Initiate();
ExecutePartTwo();
```

I already discussed that when you want to process functions sequentially, it is always better to express your intention through the code. So, you need to refactor the program. I leave this exercise to you. If you understand Demonstration 2, it will be easy for you. Otherwise, download `Exercise6.4RefactoredVersion.cs` from the Apress website.

You'll notice that in the refactored version, you cannot alter the calling sequence inside the `Execute` function, because in such cases, you'll see compile-time errors.

E6.5

True.

CHAPTER 7

Functional Patterns

Patterns are common in programming. You may use them either knowingly or unknowingly. So, what is a pattern? In simple terms, it is a description or template for solving problems that can be applied in different situations. Let me give you an example to help you understand the importance of identifying patterns. Suppose you have a requirement to write a function that can do some meaningful operation on a list. Let's further assume that you were able to solve the problem. Then you got a similar requirement for other data structures, such as an array or a dictionary. This time, you need to write a function that applies to all those data structures as well. Now you are solving the pattern of the problem, rather than the problem itself. Solving the "pattern of the problems" can give you long-term benefits. Here are some important points before you look at a detailed discussion of patterns:

- Patterns are used to solve common problems that can be repetitive. A programming language can implement many of these patterns as features.

- Patterns serve as a common vocabulary. Knowing about them can help you understand related discussions.

- Understanding patterns can make your programming life easier. If needed, you can replicate the idea to solve a problem where you do not have support for ready-made patterns (or, features). For example, in the List<T> class, you see a built-in method called ForEach that performs a specified action on each element of List<T>. Until now, Microsoft has not provided any such method for the Dictionary class or other data structures that implement IEnumerable. If you understand the implementation, you can make a similar function to traverse another data structure.

© Vaskaran Sarcar 2023
V. Sarcar, *Introducing Functional Programming Using C#*, https://doi.org/10.1007/978-1-4842-9697-4_7

- A pattern can have different names. For example, you'll learn about Map in this chapter. In the Language Integrated Query (LINQ) code, you can see an implementation of it, called Select. I'll also discuss the Bind pattern in this chapter. LINQ has an implementation of it too; we call it SelectMany.

Note   In your functional journey, I want you to be familiar with implicitly typed local variables. So, on many occasions in this chapter, I have used the var keyword instead of explicitly defining a variable such as List<int>.

A programming language can have a readymade implementation for a pattern, but it may call it by a different name. Once you understand the concept, the difference in names will not matter much to you. For example, if your program needs to pick up certain names from a list of names, your job is to write (or use) the correct function for it; it does not matter whether you refer to it by calling the name Select or Map.

Author's note   Obviously, if you use a built-in construct, you are forced to use that name only.

This chapter helps you recognize the useful functions that follow some common patterns in functional programming.

Map Pattern

In Chapter 2, I used the word *function* and *map* interchangeably. Now I am discussing the Map design pattern. To avoid any confusion, I will use the word *transform* instead of *map* in a similar context. In addition, to make the upcoming discussion easier, I will use the arrow notation. To illustrate these points, let me give you an example:

Instead of writing the following line:

Let's assume that there is a function f that **maps** an int into a string.

I will write the following:

Let's assume that there is a function f that **transforms** an int into a string.

To make it even shorter, I'll use the arrow notation:

```
f: int-> string
```

The following examples can give you the idea of how to represent a function signature using the arrow notation:

- The Func<int, string> type has the signature int->string.

- Func<int, double, string> has the signature (int,double)->string.

- In Chapter 2 you saw that the Action delegates encapsulate methods that have the void return type. So, Action<int, int> has the signature (int, int)->().

Understanding the Problem

To illustrate the importance of the Map pattern, let's look at the following problem set:

Problem 1: Given a list of numbers, display the content of the list.

Problem 2: Given a list of numbers, display the square of the numbers.

Problem 3: Increase each element of an integer list by 3.

Problem 4: Given a list of names, print the names in uppercase.

Now let me ask you the question, have you noticed any common pattern in these tasks?

Initial Solution

I know that you can find the commonality: in each case, you need to deal with a list and apply the required action (using a function that does the transformation). Once you apply the function to each element of the list, you may want to store the transformed value inside another list.

To solve these specific problems, instead of writing individual solutions, you want to incorporate a general solution. So, you can write the following extension method and use it per your needs:

```
public static List<TResult> Map<TSource, TResult>(this
  List<TSource> container, Func<TSource, TResult> f)
  {
    List<TResult> output = new();
    foreach (var item in container)
    {
```

```
      output.Add(f(item));
    }
  return output;
}
```

You can replace the `foreach` loop with the `ForEach` function to provide a more functional look, as follows:

```
public static List<TResult> Map<TSource,TResult>(
 this List<TSource> container,Func<TSource,TResult> f)
  {
    List<TResult> output = new();
    container.ForEach(item=>output.Add(f(item)));
    return outputList;
  }
```

Now you can pass the necessary function to the initial/original list to get a list with transformed values. Here is a sample usage:

```
List<int> input = Enumerable.Range(1, 5).ToList();
WriteLine("Making square of each element:");
var newList = input.Map(x => x * x);
```

So, what is the advantage of this? You can change the function to fulfill a new requirement. For example, to increase each number in the original list by 3, you can use the following line:

```
newList = input.Map(x => x + 3);
```

Congratulations! You have seen an implementation of the Map pattern. Wikipedia (see `https://en.wikipedia.org/wiki/Map_(higher-order_function)`) defines this pattern as follows:

> *In many programming languages, map is the name of a higher-order function that applies a given function to each element of a collection, e.g. a list or set, returning the results in a collection of the same type. It is often called apply-to-all when considered in functional form.*

It is time for a demonstration to clarify whether the Map pattern solves the problem set that I just discussed.

Demonstration 1

Here is a sample program for your reference. To see the complete program, you can download the project Demo1_MapPattern from the Apress website.

```
using CustomLibrary;
using System.ComponentModel;
using static System.Console;

List<int> input = Enumerable.Range(1, 5).ToList();
WriteLine("The original list contains:");
input.ForEach(x => WriteLine(x));

#region using Map
WriteLine("Making a square of each element:");
input.Map(x => x * x)
     .ForEach(x => WriteLine(x));

WriteLine("Increasing each number in the list by 3:");
input.Map(x => x + 3)
     .ForEach(x => WriteLine(x));

List<string> names = new() { "Sam", "Jack", "Joseph" };
WriteLine("Names in uppercase:");
names.Map(x => x.ToUpper())
     .ForEach(x => WriteLine(x));
#endregion

namespace CustomLibrary
{
  public static class Extensions
  {
    // The Map function is defined here
  }
}
```

> **Note**   For better clarity, I have used statements such as `input.ForEach(x =>` `WriteLine(x));`. This can be simplified by removing the lambda expression and using `input.ForEach(WriteLine);`. In the upcoming demonstrations, I'll use this simplified form.

Output

Here is the output of the program:

```
The original list contains:
1
2
3
4
5
Making a square of each element:
1
4
9
16
25
Increasing each number in the list by 3:
4
5
6
7
8
Names in uppercase:
SAM
JACK
JOSEPH
```

Better Solution

Take another look at the previously defined Map function. It is an extension method that can work with a list. We know that List<T> is a class that implements IEnumerable<T>. We also know that programming to an interface is always a better idea. So, I will show you an alternative version of Map, called Map2, that is as follows (notice the key changes in bold):

```
public static IEnumerable<TResult> Map2<TSource, TResult>(
this IEnumerable<TSource> container, Func<TSource, TResult> f)
{
    List<TResult> output = new();
    foreach (var item in container)
    {
      output.Add(f(item));
    }
    return output;
}
```

Here is a sample usage of Map2:

```
WriteLine("Making square of each element:");
input.Map2(x => x * x)
    .ToList()
    .ForEach(x => WriteLine(x));
```

Notice that this time I need to call ToList() before I call ForEach. The reason is obvious: the ForEach function is available for the List<T> class, but not for the IEnumerable<T> interface. But mentioned, your own version of ForEach in Demonstration 4 in Chapter 2 showed how to use an extension method to make a custom ForEach to traverse the dictionary elements.

Author's note The same comment applies to the upcoming solution (when I use the Map3 function) too.

Concise Solution

Since Map2 works on IEnumerable<T>, you can make the solution more concise using yield return. This construct provides the following benefits:

- It enables you to return values without specifying a type in the function body of the return value.

- It promotes deferred execution.

Here is another alternative to the Map (or Map2) function:

```
public static IEnumerable<TResult> Map3<TSource, TResult>(
 this IEnumerable<TSource> container, Func<TSource, TResult> f)
{
  foreach (var item in container)
    yield return f(item);
}
```

This indicates that you can describe the Map3(Or, Map2) function's signature with the arrow notation as follows:

```
Map3:(IEnumerable<TSource>,TSource->TResult)->IEnumerable<TResult>
```

Q&A Session

7.1 Why do you use arrow notation to represent functions? Is it mandatory?

No. But it makes the discussion easy. In mathematics, you will often see this notation to represent functions. For me, it is more readable compared to the C# type. In addition, the documentation at https://en.wikipedia.org/wiki/Function_(mathematics)#Arrow_notation points out the following advantage: "Arrow notation defines the rule of a function inline, without requiring a name to be given to the function." This is why I can use this notation in the discussion of anonymous functions or lambda expressions too.

7.2 Why do you promote deferred execution using `yield return`?

After providing some custom solutions to the problems, I'll show you how to use built-in functions from the System.Linq namespace in C#. Those functions promote deferred execution. Microsoft (see https://learn.microsoft.com/en-us/dotnet/standard/linq/deferred-execution-lazy-evaluation) says the following:

> *The LINQ technologies make extensive use of deferred execution in both the members of core System.Linq classes and in the extension methods in the various LINQ namespaces, such as System.Xml.Linq.Extensions.*

This link continues with this:

> *Deferred execution is supported directly in the C# language by the yield (C# Reference) keyword (in the form of the yield-return statement) when used within an iterator block. Such an iterator must return a collection of type IEnumerator or IEnumerator<T> (or a derived type).*

7.3 Is there any way to visualize that yield return defers an execution?

This answer requires me to show you some code snippets. Before I show them, note that I have used the Map3 and Map2 functions in the following program.

Note Since you have already seen these functions, I have not shown their definition again in this answer. You can download the complete program (Demo_ UnderstandingDeferredExecution.cs) from the Apress website and verify the answer.

```
using CustomLibrary;
using static System.Console;

WriteLine("Understanding deferred execution.");
var input = Enumerable.Range(1, 5);
var output1 = input.Map3(x => x * x);
var output2 = input.Map2(x => x * x);
```

```
// output1 is not computed yet
// but output 2 is computed already.
foreach (int i in output1)
{
    WriteLine(i);
}
foreach (int j in output2)
{
    WriteLine(j);
}

namespace CustomLibrary
{
    public static class Extensions
    {
     // Remaining code is skipped
     // Map2 and Map3 are defined here.
    }
}
```

Now I put a breakpoint on line 11 (just after using Map3 and Map2 as shown in Figure 7-1) and start debugging the program. See the status of output1 and output2 in the Watch window.

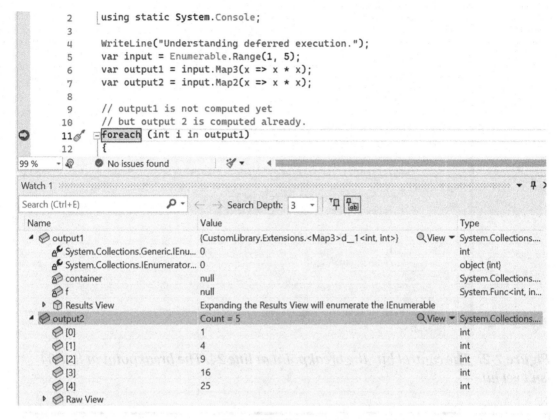

Figure 7-1. *Analyzing deferred execution using yield return*

Notice that `output2` is already computed, whereas `output1` is not computed yet. The reason is obvious: `output1` is used in line 6, which uses the `Map3` function, which in turn uses the `yield return` statement. But this did not happen with `output2`, because it uses the `Map2` function, which uses a normal `return` statement.

In fact, if you put breakpoints in these function bodies, you can observe that before the control comes to line 12, `Map2` is executed. The arrow in Figure 7-2 demonstrates this scenario.

```
10        // but output 2 and output3 is computed already.
11      ⊟foreach (int i in output1)
12       {
13            WriteLine(i);
14       }
15      ⊞foreach (int j in output2)[...]
19      ⊟namespace CustomLibrary
20       {
              0 references
21      ⊟        public static class Extensions
22               {
                     1 reference
23      ⊟            public static IEnumerable<TResult> Map2<TSource, TResult>(this IEnumer;
24                   {
25                       List<TResult> output = new();
26      ⊟                foreach (var item in container)
27                       {
28                           output.Add(f(item));
29                       }
30                       return output;
31                   }
32                   // using yield return
                     1 reference
33      ⊟            public static IEnumerable<TResult> Map3<TSource, TResult>(this IEnumer;
34                   {
```

Figure 7-2. *The control hits the breakpoint at line 24. The breakpoint at line 34 isn't yet hit*

POINT TO REMEMBER

Using yield return indicates that you are working with an iterator code block. If, by mistake, you replace the return type of Map3 from IEnumerable<TResult> to List<TResult>, you will see the following compile-time error:

CS1624 The body of 'Extensions.Map3<TSource, TResult>(IList<TSource>, Func<TSource, TResult>)' cannot be an iterator block because 'List<TResult>' is not an iterator interface type

---

Select As Map

The Select function has two overloaded versions in the System.Linq namespace. I will pick the simplest definition for your reference.

```
namespace System.Linq
{
```

```
public static partial class Enumerable
{
 public static IEnumerable<TResult> Select<TSource, TResult>(
   this IEnumerable<TSource> source,
    Func<TSource, TResult> selector)
       {
          // The remaining code is skipped
```

Note   I assume you know how to see (or debug) .NET source code. If you are unaware of this activity, you can get help from `https://learn.microsoft.com/en-us/aspnet/core/test/debug-aspnetcore-source?view=aspnetcore-7.0`.

So, in this case, we can describe the Select function with the arrow notation as follows:

`Select:(IEnumerable<TSource>,TSource->TResult)->IEnumerable<TResult>`

Notice that the signatures of Map3 and Select are identical.

POINT TO NOTE

LINQ users in C# can use either query syntax or method syntax. They are semantically identical. Many people like to use query syntax. But in this chapter, I'll use method syntax. This is because Microsoft (see `https://learn.microsoft.com/en-us/dotnet/csharp/programming-guide/concepts/linq/query-syntax-and-method-syntax-in-linq`) says the following:

However, the query syntax must be translated into method calls for the .NET common language runtime (CLR) when the code is compiled. These method calls invoke the standard query operators, which have names such as Where, Select, GroupBy, Join, Max, and Average. You can call them directly by using method syntax instead of query syntax.

The documentation continues as follows:

Some queries must be expressed as method calls. For example, you must use a method call to express a query that retrieves the number of elements that match a specified condition.

Demonstration 2

When you download the project Demo1_MapPattern from the Apress website, you'll see the usage of all of the functions: Map, Map2, and Map3. To investigate how the Select function works, let's replace all the occurrences of Map2 (or, Map3) in Demonstration 1 with Select as follows:

```
using static System.Console;

List<int> input = Enumerable.Range(1, 5).ToList();
WriteLine("The list contains:");
input.ForEach(WriteLine);

WriteLine("Making a square of each element:");
input.Select(x => x * x)
    .ToList()
    .ForEach(WriteLine);

WriteLine("Increasing each number in the original list by 3:");
input.Select(x => x + 3)
    .ToList()
    .ForEach(WriteLine);

List<string> names = new() { "Sam", "Jack", "Joseph" };
WriteLine("Names in uppercase:");
names.Select(x => x.ToUpper())
    .ToList()
    .ForEach(x => WriteLine(x.ToUpper()));
```

Note I used the built-in Select function in Demonstration 2. So, there was no need to create (or use) a custom extension method such as Map, Map2, or Map3.

Once you run this program, you'll see the same output that you saw in Demonstration 1. I do not repeat it here.

Q&A Session

7.4 Does Select promote deferred execution?

Yes.

7.5 In the Microsoft implementation of Select, I can see some additional checks such as the following:

```
public static IEnumerable<TResult> Select<TSource, TResult>(
  this IEnumerable<TSource> source,
      Func<TSource, TResult> selector)
      {
          if (source == null)
          {
              // Some code skipped
          }

          if (selector == null)
          {
              // Some code skipped
          }
          // Remaining code is skipped
```

But in your implementations, I do not see them. Is there any specific reason for this?

I showed you the core implementations that are easy to understand. If you need to consider all possible corner cases, the overall discussions can be boring as well as complex. Do not forget that, ultimately, I'll be using built-in functions such as Select, SelectMany, and Where in this chapter. These predefined functions save development time and improve performance. But as mentioned at the beginning of this chapter, I want you to understand the patterns that these built-in functions follow, instead of blindly using them as features.

Introducing Functors

Before I introduce functors, let's review the Map function:

- In functional programming (FP), you will often notice that Map is implemented as a higher-order function (HOF).

- A Map function has at least two parameters: a data container and a function.

- Usually, the function is represented by a delegate (or a lambda).

- You apply this function to each item in the container and get another container that holds the transformed data.

The container that has such a Map function is called a **functor**.

Conclusion

You can see that the behavior of Select and Map3 are identical. The LINQ programmers know this. In fact, C# developers consider Select as an implementation of the Map pattern, and they treat Map and Select as synonyms. Most importantly, since I used the built-in Select function in Demonstration 2, there was no need to create an extension method. As a result, this program is shorter, simpler, and easy to maintain.

POINT TO NOTE

Often you see the same construct with different names. You have already seen examples where the Map and Select functions are equivalent. In addition to the common names such as Select and Map, if you notice a different name such as Project, you should not be surprised. This is because you can always choose a meaningful name for your function. I told you earlier that different programming languages can use different names to implement the same pattern. So, you should not wonder when you hear C# developers using the word Select and Map interchangeably.

Q&A Session

7.6 You have explored the Map function for IEnumerable<T>. Is it possible to define a common signature for this function?

Yes. Though we have explored the Map function for IEnumerable<T>, this function can be defined for other types as well. Following the signature of Select (or Map2 or Map3), you can define a common and concise signature for the Map pattern. How? Let's replace IEnumerable with C (the first letter of "Container"), TSource with T, and TResult with R. As a result, the signature of the Map function can be defined as follows:

Map:(C<T>,T->R)->C<R>

You may notice that the Map pattern has a simple generic definition. As a result, a generic type can implement it easily.

7.7 Can you give an example of a functor?

You have seen that the Select is a Map function that is implemented as an extension method of IEnumerable<TSource>. So, we can say that IEnumerable is a functor.

Bind Pattern

Bind is another important pattern, but it is a little bit complex compared to Map. To explain the Map pattern, I followed these steps:

1. I started with a set of problems to help you understand the importance of identifying a pattern.

2. Initially, I showed you some custom solutions.

3. In the end, I used the built-in Select function, and in using it, I made the code shorter and cleaner. In fact, since Select is a built-in function, you can expect it to be more optimized.

I'll follow similar steps to discuss the Bind pattern.

Understanding the Problem

Let's begin with a problem. You know that a company has various departments, and each employee has a unique ID. To represent a department, let's define the following type:

```
class Department
{
    public string Name { get; set; }
    public List<string> Ids { get; set; }
}
```

Look at the following code segment where the sales department has two employees with the IDs S1 and S2 and the production department has three employees with IDs the P1, P2, and P3:

```
var salesDept = new Department {
                Name = "Sales",
                Ids = new List<string> { "S1", "S2" }
                };
var productDept = new Department {
                Name = "Production",
                Ids =new List<string> { "P1", "P2", "P3" }
                };
```

For simplicity, let's assume that the company has only these departments. Since the company consists of these two departments, you'll see the following code in the upcoming program:

```
var company = new List<Department> { salesDept, productDept };
```

Earlier you solved problems 1 to 4 using the Map pattern. This time I'll give you another problem to solve. Here it is:

Problem 5: Can you select all the employee IDs in this company?

Initial Solution

You can solve this problem in various ways. For example, a developer can write the following lines:

```
// Imperative style
var salesIds = salesDept.Ids;
var productIds = productDept.Ids;
var allIds=salesIds.Concat(productIds);
```

```
foreach(var id in allIds)
{
    WriteLine(id);
}
```

But this does not follow the functional style of coding. Let's search for another solution.

FP-Based Solution

If you want to follow the functional style, you can write the following extension method:

```
public static IEnumerable<TResult> Bind<TSource, TResult>(
    this IEnumerable<TSource> container,
    Func<TSource, IEnumerable<TResult>> f)
    {
      foreach (var outerItem in container)
       foreach (var innerItem in f(outerItem))
        yield return innerItem;
    }
```

Note   You saw the advantage of using `yield return` when I discussed the concise solution for the Map pattern.

Use it as follows:

```
WriteLine("Using the custom function-Bind");
company.Bind(x => x.Ids)
      .ToList()
      .ForEach(WriteLine);
```

Let's verify whether this Bind function can help us to solve the problem.

Demonstration 3

Here is a sample program for your reference. To see the complete program, you can download the project Demo3_BindPattern from the Apress website.

```
using CustomLibrary;
using static System.Console;

WriteLine("Testing the bind pattern.");
var salesDept = new Department {
  Name = "Sales",
  Ids = new List<string> { "S1", "S2" }
 };

var productDept = new Department {
  Name = "Production",
  Ids = new List<string> { "P1", "P2", "P3" }
 };

var company = new List<Department> { salesDept, productDept };
WriteLine("The company has assigned the following ids:");

company.Bind(x => x.Ids)
       .ToList()
       .ForEach(WriteLine);

class Department
{
    public string Name { get; set; }
    public List<string> Ids { get; set; }
}

namespace CustomLibrary
{
  public static class Extensions
   {
     // The Bind function is defined here
   }
}
```

Output

Here is the output of the program:

```
Testing the bind pattern.
The company has assigned the following ids:
S1
S2
P1
P2
P3
```

SelectMany As Bind

Here is the definition of the SelectMany function from the System.Linq namespace:

```
public static IEnumerable<TResult> SelectMany<TSource,TResult>
 (
  this IEnumerable<TSource> source,
  Func<TSource,IEnumerable<TResult>> selector)
  {
  //...
```

So, in this case, we can describe the SelectMany function with the arrow notation as follows:

```
SelectMany:(IEnumerable<TSource>,
            TSource->IEnumerable<TResult>)->
            IEnumerable<TResult>
```

Notice that the signatures of Bind and SelectMany are identical. To investigate how the SelectMany function works, let's replace the Bind function in Demonstration 3 with the built-in SelectMany function.

Demonstration 4

Here is the updated program:

```
using static System.Console;
```

```
WriteLine("Testing the bind pattern.");
var salesDept = new Department { Name = "Sales", Ids = new List<string> {
  "S1", "S2" } };
var productDept = new Department { Name = "Production", Ids = new
  List<string> { "P1", "P2", "P3" } };
var company = new List<Department> { salesDept, productDept };
WriteLine("The company has assigned the following ids:");
company.SelectMany(x => x.Ids)
        .ToList()
        .ForEach(x => WriteLine(x));

class Department
{
    public string Name { get; set; }
    public List<string> Ids { get; set; }
}
```

Note   I used the built-in SelectMany function in Demonstration 4. So, there was no need to create (or use) an extension method.

Once you run this program, you'll see the same output that you saw in Demonstration 3. I do not repeat it here.

What About Monads?

After the discussion of the Map pattern, I discussed functors.

Similar to Map and functors, you will hear about Bind and monads together. In fact, in many books or articles, you'll see the discussion of monads after the Bind pattern. But I want to discuss some key constructs before I discuss monads. So, I have kept the discussion of monads in a separate chapter (Chapter 9).

Conclusion

The behavior of Bind and SelectMany is identical. In fact, C# developers consider SelectMany as an implementation of the Bind pattern, and they treat SelectMany and Bind as synonyms. Most importantly, since I used the built-in SelectMany function in Demonstration 4, there was no need to create an extension method. As a result, this program is shorter and simpler.

In this section, I discussed the flattening aspect of the Bind pattern. You saw me demonstrate this pattern with the built-in function called SelectMany. My goal was to make a one-dimensional list from a nested list; in other words, I "flattened" a list. This is one of the reasons many developers prefer to call this pattern FlatMap instead of Bind.

Q&A Session

7.8 You explored the Bind function for IEnumerable<T>. Is it possible to define a common signature for this function?

Yes. Though we have explored the Bind function for IEnumerable<T>, this function can be defined for other types as well. Following the signature of SelectMany, we can define a common and concise signature for the Bind pattern. How? Let's replace the IEnumerable with C (the first letter of "Container"), TSource with T, and TResult with R. As a result, the signature of the Bind function can be defined as follows:

Bind:(C<T>,T->C<R>)->C<R>

7.9 You have mentioned the flattening aspect of the Bind pattern. Does this indicate that the SelectMany function can be used in a different scenario too?

Yes. You can use it to find the Cartesian product (cross-join) of two lists. For example, consider the following code (the use of the SelectMany function is highlighted in bold):

```
using static System.Console;
WriteLine("Using the SelectMany function for joining lists.");
var setA = Enumerable.Range(1, 2).ToList();
var setB = Enumerable.Range(3, 3).ToList();
WriteLine("\nThe set A contains :");
setA.ForEach(x => Write(x+"\t"));

WriteLine("\nThe set B contains:");
setB.ForEach(x => Write(x+"\t"));
```

```
WriteLine("\nThe cartesian product:");
setA.SelectMany(x => setB.Select(y =>$"({x},{y})"))
    .ToList()
    .ForEach(x=>Write(x+"\t"));
```

This code produces the following output:

```
Using the SelectMany function for joining lists.

The set A contains :
1       2
The set B contains:
3       4       5
The cartesian product:
(1,3)   (1,4)   (1,5)   (2,3)   (2,4)   (2,5)
```

Note   You can download the file Demo_SelectManyAsJoin.cs from the Apress website to test this program.

Filter Pattern

The next functional pattern I'll discuss is called Filter. It is another useful pattern in FP.

Understanding the Problem

Earlier, to illustrate the importance of patterns, I gave you some problems. We solved problems 1 to 4 using the Map pattern. You saw solutions to problem 5 using the Bind pattern. Here is another set of problems:

Problem 6: Given a list of integers, display the even numbers.
Problem 7: Given an array of floating-point numbers, pick the numbers that are greater than 50.2.
Problem 8: Given a list of names, print the names that start with "S" or the names that contain more than three characters.

Initial Solution

You can solve these problems in various ways. Have you noticed any common pattern in these assignments? If not, let me highlight the important points as follows:

- These problems are based on arrays and lists.

- Each case demands you filter out the unwanted values. In other words, you accept only those values that meet a certain condition.

- The previous step produces values that are basically a subset of the original values.

So, instead of writing code to solve these specific problems for a list or an array, you want to incorporate a general solution that can work for both. You can write the following extension method and use it per your needs:

```
public static IEnumerable<T> Filter<T>(this IEnumerable<T>
    container, Func<T, bool> f)
    {
        foreach (var item in container)
        {
            if (f(item))
            {
                yield return item;
            }
        }
    }
```

Note   You saw the advantage of using **yield return** when I discussed the concise solution for the Map pattern.

---

you can use it as follows (notice the bold line):

```
WriteLine("\nThe even numbers are:");
integers
    .Filter(x => x % 2 == 0)
    .ToList()
    .ForEach(x => WriteLine(x));
```

Let's verify whether this Filter function solves the given problems.

Demonstration 5

Here is the complete program:

```
using CustomLibrary;
using static System.Console;
var integers = Enumerable.Range(1, 5).ToList();
WriteLine("The original set of integers is:");
integers.ForEach(x => Write(x + "\t"));
WriteLine("\nThe even numbers are:");
integers
    .Filter(x => x % 2 == 0)
    .ToList()
    .ForEach(WriteLine);

double[] realNumbers = { 20.25, 30.37, 40.42, 50.57, 60.75 };
WriteLine("\nThe original set of real numbers is:");
realNumbers.ToList().ForEach(x => Write(x + "\t"));
WriteLine("\nThe real numbers that are greater than 50.2 are:");
realNumbers
    .Filter(x => x > 50.2)
    .ToList()
    .ForEach(WriteLine);

var names = new() { "Sam", "Bob", "Jack", "Kate",
 "Joseph" };
WriteLine("\nThe original set of names:");
names.ForEach(x => Write(x + "\t"));
```

```
WriteLine("\nThe names that start with 'S', or contain more
 than 3 characters are:");
names
    .Filter(x => x.Length > 3 | x.StartsWith('S'))
    .ToList()
    .ForEach(WriteLine);

namespace CustomLibrary
{
    public static class Extensions
    {
        // The Filter function is defined here
    }
}
```

Output

Here is the output of the program:

```
The original set of integers is:
1       2       3       4       5
The even numbers are:
2
4

The original set of real numbers is:
20.25   30.37   40.42   50.57   60.75
The real numbers that are greater than 50.2 are:
50.57
60.75

The original set of names:
Sam     Bob     Jack    Kate    Joseph
The names that start with `S', or contain more than 3
 characters are:
Sam
Jack
Kate
Joseph
```

Where As Filter

Here is the definition of the Where function from the System.Linq namespace:

```
public static IEnumerable<TSource> Where<TSource>(
  this IEnumerable<TSource> source, Func<TSource,
  bool> predicate)
{
 // Remaining code skipped
```

So, in this case, you can describe the Where function with the arrow notation as follows:

```
Where:(IEnumerable<TSource>, TSource->bool)->IEnumerable<Source>
```

For your reference, here is the definition of the Filter function from Demonstration 5:

```
public static IEnumerable<T> Filter<T>(
 this IEnumerable<T> container,
 Func<T, bool> f)
{
// Remaining code skipped
```

So, in this case, you can describe the Filter function with the arrow notation as follows:

```
Filter:(IEnumerable<T>, T->bool)->IEnumerable<T>
```

Demonstration 6

Notice that the signatures of Filter and Where are identical. To investigate the working mechanism of the Where function, let's replace all occurrences of Filter in Demonstration 5 with Where in a separate program and execute it. You'll get the exact same output. As usual, since you are using the built-in function Where in this program (Demonstration 6), you do not need to create a custom extension method. So, Demonstration 6 will be shorter and simpler compared to Demonstration 5. This time, I will not repeat the whole program. You can download the project (Demo6_UsingWhere) from the Apress website.

Conclusion

You can see that the behavior of Filter and Where is identical. Again, LINQ users probably know about this already. This is why C# developers consider Where as an implementation of the Filter pattern and they often treat Filter and Where as synonyms. As usual, when you use the built-in Where function, there is no need to create an extension method. As a result, the program will be shorter and simpler too.

Fold Pattern

Now I'll discuss another important functional pattern, called Fold. Wikipedia (https://en.wikipedia.org/wiki/Fold_(higher-order_function)) states the following:

In functional programming, fold (also termed reduce, accumulate, aggregate, compress, or inject) refers to a family of higher-order functions that analyze a recursive data structure and through use of a given combining operation, recombine the results of recursively processing its constituent parts, building up a return value.

For example, suppose you have the list [1,2,3]. To calculate the sum of the elements of the list, you will perform the operation 1+2+3. But instead of calculating the result in a single shot, you can carry out the calculations in different ways. For example:

- You can add the first two elements (1 and 2) and get an intermediate result (3). Then you add the third element (3) to this intermediate result to compute the result. Using parentheses, you can denote it as (1+2) +3.

- Alternatively, you can add the last two elements (2 and 3) to get an intermediate result (5). Then you add the first element (1) to this intermediate result. Using parentheses, you can denote it as 1+(2+3). This is why the previous online link says this:

*On lists, there are two obvious ways to carry this out: either by combining the first element with the result of recursively combining the rest (called a **right fold**), or by combining the result of recursively combining all elements but the last one, with the last element (called a **left fold**).*

- Now you understand the difference between the left fold and the right fold. For example, $(((1+2)+3)+4)$ is an example of the left fold, and $(1+(2+(3+4)))$ is an example of the right fold.

The concept is not limited to integer additions. The same concept can be applied to other operations such as concatenating strings or multiplying numbers. For example, to calculate the factorial of a number, you can apply this pattern. To illustrate this, let me show you a code fragment where I calculate the factorial of 6 using the Aggregate function as follows:

```
using static System.Console;
WriteLine("\nFinding the factorial of 6.");
int factorial = Enumerable
    .Range(1, 6)
    .Aggregate((x, y) =>
    {
        // Showing the intermediate values
        WriteLine($"Current:{x}, Next:{y}, Temp: {x*y}");
        return x * y;
    }
    );
WriteLine($"The factorial of 6 is:{ factorial}");
```

Once you compile and run this code, you'll see the following output:

```
Finding the factorial of 6.
Current:1, Next:2, Temp: 2
Current:2, Next:3, Temp: 6
Current:6, Next:4, Temp: 24
Current:24, Next:5, Temp: 120
Current:120, Next:6, Temp: 720
The factorial of 6 is:720
```

You can see that initially, I multiplied the first two elements (1 and 2), and the result (2) is multiplied by the third element (3). The same process is continued until the end. To visualize this, I show you the values under the headings of Current, Next, and Temp.

From the output, one thing is certain: the built-in Aggregate function is doing a left fold. Interestingly, you won't find any built-in support for the right fold. But if you ever worked with MoreLINQ, you'll see that it has support for the right fold. GitHub (https://github.com/morelinq/MoreLINQ) describes this as follows:

Applies a right-associative accumulator function over a sequence. This operator is the right-associative version of the Aggregate LINQ operator.

This method has 3 overloads.

Note   I have not used MoreLINQ in this book. This is because the topics I targeted were nicely covered with the built-in features of C# and the two additional libraries Curryfy and language-ext. But I must say that MoreLINQ is a popular library, and many C# developers use it often to get helpful extensions for LINQ. You can find more information about it at https://morelinq.github.io/.

While applying the Fold pattern, the choice of the initial value is often important. For example, choosing 0 as an initial value is OK for the addition operations. This is because you can think $1 + (2 + (3 + (4 + (5 + 0))))$ as an example of the right fold, and think of it as $((((0 + 1) + 2) + 3) + 4) + 5$ for the left fold. But you cannot choose 0 as the initial value for the multiplication operation. So, while calculating the factorial, you'll choose the initial value 1, not 0.

To illustrate the importance of this, I'll use the Aggregate function again. At the time of this writing, it has three overloads. In two of these overloaded versions, you can choose a seed value. For example, to calculate **10 times the factorial of 5**, you can choose the seed value 10. Here is a sample:

```
WriteLine("\nFinding 10 times factorial of 5.");
int multiplicationResult = Enumerable
    .Range(1, 5).Aggregate(10,(x, y) =>
    {
        // Testing the intermediate values
        WriteLine($"Current:{x}, Next:{y}, Temp: {x * y}");
        return x * y;
    }
    );

WriteLine($"The final result is: {multiplicationResult}");
```

Once you compile and run this code, you'll see the following output:

```
Finding 10 times factorial of 5.
Current:10, Next:1, Temp: 10
Current:10, Next:2, Temp: 20
Current:20, Next:3, Temp: 60
Current:60, Next:4, Temp: 240
Current:240, Next:5, Temp: 1200
The final result is: 1200
```

You can see that the seed value is multiplied by 1 at the beginning, and then the result is multiplied by 2. A similar process continues until I process the last element (in this case, 5). I hope that you now have an idea of the fold pattern. Let's investigate a few more uses of this pattern with a complete demonstration.

Understanding the Problem

Earlier, to illustrate the importance of patterns, I gave you some problems. We solved problems 1 to 8 using the Map pattern, Bind pattern, and Filter pattern. This time, consider the following problems:

Problem 9: Given an array of integers, find the maximum, minimum, and count of the integers.

Problem 10: Suppose you have a list of integers. Apply a function to each member of the list and show the maximum (or minimum).

Problem 11: Suppose you have a list of integers. Find the sum of the numbers that are divisible by 3.

Problem 12: Find the factorial of a given number. (You have seen a solution already.)

Solutions Using Built-in Functions

You can solve these problems in various ways. I'll repeat a question, have you noticed any common pattern in these problems? I assume that you can find it. If not, let me highlight the important points as follows:

- These problems are based on arrays and lists.

- Each case demands you get some value such as a maximum value, a minimum value, or a factorial. In short, instead of processing another list (or an array), you need to get a value. So, you need to rely on some functions that can accumulate the final value. This is why such kinds of functions are also called **accumulative functions**.

- The previous point describes the pattern: you apply a function to each item of a sequence (or collection such as a list or array), and in turn, the function returns the desired value. In the .NET world, these functions are also known as **aggregate functions**.

- Now you got the point! Using the fold pattern, you can solve these problems.

Again, instead of writing code to solve these specific problems for a list or an array, you would like to incorporate a general solution that can work for both. In the previous sections, I showed you some initial solutions using the custom functions. This time I need multiple functions to solve these problems. But LINQ provides the built-in functions to solve these problems. So, instead of solving these problems using custom functions, this time I'll use those built-in functions. These built-in functions have many overloaded versions. You have already seen two overloads of the `Aggregate` function. In the upcoming program, I'll also use the `Max` and `Sum` functions. They have the following descriptions that are easy to assume:

- `Max` finds the maximum from a given sequence.

- `Sum` computes the sum of the given sequence.

Let's look at the next demonstration.

Demonstration 7

Here is the complete program:

```
using static System.Console;

WriteLine("Understanding the fold pattern.");
var integers = Enumerable.Range(1, 10).ToArray();
```

```
WriteLine("The original set of numbers is:");
integers
    .ToList()
    .ForEach(x => Write(x + " "));

WriteLine("\nThe highest number is:");
int highest = integers.Max();
WriteLine(highest);

WriteLine("\nFinding the total of original numbers:");
int total = integers.Sum();
WriteLine(total);

WriteLine("\nMultiplying each element by -5 and now the highest
 number is:");
highest = integers.Max(x => x * (-5));
WriteLine(highest);

WriteLine("\nFinding the total of those numbers that are
 divisible by 3:");
total = integers.Where(x => x % 3 == 0).Sum();
WriteLine(total);

WriteLine("\nFinding the factorial of 6.");
int factorial = Enumerable
    .Range(1, 6)
    .Aggregate((x, y) => x * y);
WriteLine($"The factorial of 6 is:{ factorial}");
```

Output

Here is the output of the program:

```
Understanding the fold pattern.
The original set of numbers is:
1 2 3 4 5 6 7 8 9 10
The highest number is:
10
```

Finding the total of original numbers:
55

Multiplying each element by -5 and now the highest number is:
-5

Finding the total of those numbers that are divisible by 3:
18

Finding the factorial of 6.
The factorial of 6 is:720

Conclusion

I have shown you the use of the functions Max, Sum, and Aggregate. I mentioned earlier that in the .NET world, these are called **aggregate functions**. There are many built-in functions in this category such as Min(), Count(), and Average(). They have their usual meaning. You can play with these functions. I prefer to leave this exercise to you. Using the Fold pattern, you can create these aggregate functions since it is generic enough to be configured using the desired accumulator.

Q&A Session

7.10 There is no built-in support for the right fold. Does this mean that if I need the right fold, I have to use a third-party library such as MoreLINQ?

No. Look at the following expression: (1+(2+(3+4))). Here you are performing right fold. But notice that this expression can be written as follows: (((4+3)+2)+1). I am reversing the list of numbers and then applying the left fold. If needed, you can replicate this idea.

Earlier you saw that I calculated the factorial of 6 using the Aggregate function that follows the left fold mechanism. This time let me show you a sample program where I invoke the Reverse function (to invert the order of the elements in a sequence) before I call the Aggregate function, as follows:

```
using static System.Console;
int factorial2 = Enumerable
    .Range(1, 6)
    .Reverse()
```

```
    .Aggregate
    (
      (x, y) =>
        {
        // Showing the intermediate values
        WriteLine($"Current:{x}, Next:{y}, Temp: {x * y}");
        return x * y;
        }
  );
WriteLine($"The factorial of 6 is:{factorial2}");
```

This program will produce the following output:

```
Current:6, Next:5, Temp: 30
Current:30, Next:4, Temp: 120
Current:120, Next:3, Temp: 360
Current:360, Next:2, Temp: 720
Current:720, Next:1, Temp: 720
The factorial of 6 is:720
```

This is how you can mimic the idea of the right fold. You may also note that in this program, I have used the statement lambda to show you the intermediate values. If you want, you can shorten the program as follows:

```
using static System.Console;
int factorial2 =
    Enumerable
    .Range(1, 6)
    .Reverse()
    .Aggregate((x, y) => x * y);
WriteLine($"The factorial of 6 is:{factorial2}");
```

Interestingly, there is a catch! We have considered the multiplication operation here; so, everything went well. But if you consider the division operation, the result can be surprising. For example: $(1/(2/3))$ is not equal to $((3/2)/1)$. This is why a better solution can be made using a custom extension method. Here is a sample:

```
  public static TSource RightFold<TSource>(
    this IEnumerable<TSource> source,
```

```
Func<TSource, TSource, TSource> func)
  {
    return source.Reverse().Aggregate((a, b) => func(b, a));
  }
```

Using this extension method, you can also calculate the factorial as follows:

```
int factorial2 = Enumerable
               .Range(1, 6)
               .RightFold((x, y) => x * y);
```

Revisiting ForEach

Let's take a close look at the ForEach function that I used throughout this book. At the time of this writing, this function is available in the List<T> class only. So, when I needed to traverse an IEnumerable<T> other than List<T>, I needed to call ToList() to get a list before I use the ForEach function. Here is such a code fragment from Demonstration 7 in this chapter:

```
var integers = Enumerable.Range(1, 10).ToArray();
WriteLine("The original set of numbers are:");
integers
    .ToList()
    .ForEach(x => Write(x + " "));
```

If you further investigate the ForEach function, you'll see the following code in the in-built List<T> class:

```
public void ForEach(Action<T> action){
//Some code
}
```

This code fragment gives you a clue that the ForEach takes an Action<T> and works on that. This is why I defined the following extension method in Chapter 2 (see Q&A 2.3) to provide similar support for other data structures as well:

```
namespace Extensions
{
    public static class Extensions
```

```
    {
        public static void ForEach<T>(this IEnumerable<T>
          sequence, Action<T> action)
        {
            if (action != null)
            {
                foreach (T item in sequence)
                {
                    action(item);
                }
            }
        }
    }
}
```

If you have such an extension method, you do not need to invoke ToList() before you call ForEach for an IEnumerable<T>. So, instead of just seeing the ForEach as a language feature, you can try to understand the underlying pattern associated with it. The pattern says that you can apply an Action<T> instance to each item of a sequence. What is the effect? You cause side effects! But this is a desirable side effect. In fact, you can consider the ForEach function as a side-effecting variant of Map.

This was a big chapter! We covered core functional patterns with custom functions as well as built-in functions. If you were already familiar with LINQ, the content of the chapter may seem easy to understand. But remember, as I said earlier, the goal of the chapter was to make you familiar with the core functional patterns that can serve your common needs. So, rather than seeing Select, SelectMany, and other functions just as functions, try to understand the underlying pattern they support. The payoff can be huge. Understanding these patterns will make your functional journey easier and more enjoyable.

Exercises

E7.1 Can you show the usage of a function that represents the C# type ()->()?

E7.2 Can you show the usage of a function that represents the C# type (string, int)->string?

E7.3 Can you compile the following code?

```
using static System.Console;
using CustomLibrary;
WriteLine("Exercise 7.3");
var input = Enumerable.Range(10, 5);
input.Map(x => x + 5)
    .ToList()
    .ForEach(WriteLine);

namespace CustomLibrary
{
  public static class Extensions
  {
    public static IEnumerable<TResult> Map<TSource,
     TResult>(
     this IEnumerable<TSource> container,
     Func<TSource, TResult> f)
     {
           return container.Select(f);
     }
  }
}
```

E7.4 Can you define a custom bind function for IEnumerable in terms of the built-in function SelectMany?

E7.5 How do you distinguish the Map pattern from the Filter pattern?

E7.6 Can you predict the output of the following program?

```
using static System.Console;
WriteLine("Exercise 7.6");
int result = Enumerable
    .Range(1, 5)
    .Where(x => x % 2 == 1)
    .Aggregate(5, (x, y) => x * y);
WriteLine($"The result is:{result}");
```

E7.7 Can you predict the output of the following program?

```
using static System.Console;
WriteLine("Exercise 7.7");
var result = Enumerable.Range(1, 5)
                      .Select(x => Math.Pow(x, 3))
                      .Sum();
WriteLine($"The result is: {result}");
```

E7.8 Can you predict the output of the following program?

```
using static System.Console;
WriteLine("Exercise 7.8");
List<int> list1 = Enumerable.Range(1, 3).ToList();
List<int> list2 = Enumerable.Range(4, 2).ToList();
var result = list1.SelectMany(x => list2.Select(y => x * y));
result.ToList().ForEach(x=> WriteLine(x));
```

Summary

Understanding patterns and their proper usage are integral parts of programming. Functional programming also follows some common patterns. This chapter discussed them with examples. Briefly, it covered the following patterns:

- Map pattern
- Bind pattern
- Filter pattern
- Fold pattern
- ForEach pattern

Solutions to Exercises

Here are the solutions.

E7.1

Notice that there is no input or output parameter. So, `Action` can represent `()-> ()`. Here is a sample usage:

```
using static System.Console;
Action action=() => WriteLine("Hello");
action();
```

This code will produce this output: `Hello`.

E7.2

`(string, int)->string` indicates that the function accepts a string type and an `int` type and returns an `int`. So, `Func<string, int, int>` can represent this function type. Here is a sample usage:

```
using static System.Console;
Func<string,int,string> func=
 (string s,int i) => $"{s} was published in {i}";
var input=func("This book", 2023);
WriteLine(input);
```

This code will produce the output `This book was published in 2023`.

E7.3

Yes. This code can produce the following output:

```
Exercise 7.3
15
16
17
18
19
```

Here you increase each element of a list by 5. This code shows that you can define a custom `Map` function in terms of the built-in function `Select`.

E7.4

Yes. You can use the following function in Demonstration 3 to verify the result:

```
public static IEnumerable<TResult> Bind<TSource, TResult>(
 this IEnumerable<TSource> container,
 Func<TSource, IEnumerable<TResult>> f)
{
 return container.SelectMany(f);
}
```

E7.5

In Q&A 7.6, you saw that the signature of the Map function can be defined as follows:

```
Map:(C<T>, T->R)->C<R>
```

Notice that T->R is not necessarily a predicate function (a predicate function returns a Boolean value: true or false). But in the case of the Filter pattern, you have seen that it uses a predicate function. This is why you see the presence of the Func<T, bool> type in the Where function's signature.

E7.6

This program will produce the output:

```
Exercise 7.6
The result is:75
```

[Clue: 5*1*3*5=75]

E7.7

This program will produce the following output:

```
Exercise 7.7
The result is: 225
```

[Clue: 1+8+27+64+125=225]

E7.8

This program will produce the following output:

```
Exercise 7.8
4 5 8 10 12 15
```

[Clue: 1*4=4,1*5=5,2*4=8,2*5=10,3*4=12,3*5=15]

CHAPTER 8

Exception Handling

When you write code for an application, you expect that it will execute per your plan, but sometimes you encounter sudden surprises. These surprises may occur because of some careless mistake such as you implementing the wrong logic, you ignoring some loopholes in the code paths of the program, etc. However, many software failures are beyond the control of a programmer. Developers often call these unwanted situations *exceptions*, and handling them is essential when you create an application.

Reviewing Exception Handling in OOP

In Chapter 1, you learned that most mainstream languages, including C#, primarily support imperative programming with try, catch, and throw statements. The keywords try, catch, and finally are typically absent in the functional style of coding. This is because they interrupt the execution flow, which is a side effect. In fact, you may have even heard the advice that you should not use exceptions to control the flow of execution. This is why functional programming (FP) likes to handle errors as little as possible.

I have written chapters on exception handling in my other books that were dedicated to object-oriented programming (OOP), but this chapter does not go into detail. Instead, after giving a quick overview of exception handling in OOP, this chapter will show you some alternative FP-based approaches to deal with exceptions.

Honestly, in FP, you can handle errors in several different ways. In this chapter, I'll primarily handle them using the Either type, which follows the FP pattern and is available in the language-ext library. But before you see those examples, let's quickly review exception handling in the traditional OOP style. We will compare the imperative style of error handling to the functional style of error handling.

© Vaskaran Sarcar 2023
V. Sarcar, *Introducing Functional Programming Using C#*, https://doi.org/10.1007/978-1-4842-9697-4_8

In OOP, you typically use the following keywords to deal with C# exceptions: `try`, `catch`, `throw`, and `finally`. In addition, starting with C# 6.0, you can use the contextual keyword `when` in a `catch` statement to filter an exception. Here I summarize their usage:

- You can guard an exception using a `try-catch` block. The code that may throw an exception is placed inside a `try` block, and this exceptional situation is handled inside a `catch` block.

- The code in the `finally` block must execute. In general, this block is placed after a `try` block or a `try-catch` block.

- When an exception is raised inside a `try` block, the control jumps to the respective `catch` or `finally` block. The remaining part of the `try` block will not be executed.

- You can associate multiple `catch` blocks with a `try` block. In this case, you must place them from the most specific to the least specific types.

- In addition, anyone can raise an exception with the `throw` keyword. Here is some sample code for you:

  ```
  try
  {
      // Some code before
      throw new IndexOutOfRangeException("Some message.");
      // Other code, if any
  }
  // Remaining code, if any
  ```

- Finally, as mentioned, you can use exception filters that allow you to catch an exception when a certain condition is met. For now, let me show you a sample code segment to demonstrate this:

  ```
  catch (Exception ex) when (ex.Message.Contains("Timeout"))
  {
      Console.WriteLine($"Caught: " + ex.Message);
  }
  ```

Author's note All C# exceptions are runtime exceptions. So, there is no concept of compile-time checked exceptions. This was a design decision.

Imperative Style of Programming

Enough review! Let's start analyzing a simple program that uses a function (GetQuotient) to perform a division operation. Later, I display the result. Invoking this function can cause a runtime exception to occur, so you guard the call using a try-catch block of statements.

Note   Earlier you saw me use separate namespaces for the extension methods and custom libraries. When you make a class public, the Visual Studio IDE also suggests that you place the types in a separate namespace. In general, this looks cleaner, but you need to maintain the additional indentation. As you progress through this chapter, the programs will be bigger, and the additional indentations can cause difficulties for readers, particularly when reading code in a book. I am already using top-level statements. To remove the additional indentations, I will not use separate namespaces for the programs in this chapter. The same comment applies to the remaining content of this book.

Demonstration 1

Here is the complete program:

```
using OopCsharp;
using static System.Console;

WriteLine("***Case study on exception handling in OOP.***");
int dividend = new Random().Next(10, 12);
int divisor = new Random().Next(3);
WriteLine($"Dividend: {dividend}, Divisor: {divisor}");
int quotient = 0;

try
{
    quotient = Calculator.GetQuotient(dividend, divisor);
}
catch (Exception e)
{
```

```
    WriteLine($"Error: {e}");
}

WriteLine($"Quotient: {quotient}");

class Calculator
{
    public static int GetQuotient(int a, int b) => a / b;
}
```

Output

Here is a sample output (there is no exception):

```
***Case study on exception handling in OOP.***
Dividend: 10, Divisor: 1
Quotient: 10
```

Here is more sample output (with the exception):

```
***Case study on exception handling in OOP.***
Dividend: 11, Divisor: 0
Error: System.DivideByZeroException: Attempted to divide by zero.
   at OopCsharp.Calculator.GetQuotient(Int32 a, Int32 b) in E:\MyPrograms\
FunctionalC#\ErrorHandlingSolution\Demo1_OOPExceptionHandling\Program.
cs:line 25
   at Program.<Main>$(String[] args) in E:\MyPrograms\FunctionalC#\
ErrorHandlingSolution\Demo1_OOPExceptionHandling\Program.cs:line 12
Quotient: 0
```

Exception Handling in FP

You have learned that FP likes to work with honest functions. Did you notice that in Demonstration 1, the GetQuotient function is dishonest? Why? It was supposed to perform a division operation with two integers and return the correct result (that is, an int type). But, when the divisor is zero, it raises an exception, and ultimately, you get an incorrect result.

Using language-ext

Now the question is, how can you make the GetQuotient function honest when there are two possible outcomes? This is where the Either type can help you. In our case, the GetQuotient function can either return the correct result (which is an int) or raise an exception. So, you can use Either<Exception,int> as the return type of this function. To get this type, I'll use the language-ext library.

Note   It is standard practice to put the error on the left side and the correct value on the right side. So, you will see Either<Exception,int>, but not Either<int,Exception>.

Introducing the Either Type

You can understand the Either type by looking at some examples. Before you see the examples, I'll show you some definitions behind this type.

Let's first verify the concept using a purely functional language such as Haskell. The online documentation (https://hackage.haskell.org/package/category-extras-0.52.1/docs/Control-Monad-Either.html) says the following:

> *The Either type represents values with two possibilities: a value of type Either a b is either Left a or Right b. The Either type is sometimes used to represent a value which is either correct or an error; by convention, the Left constructor is used to hold an error value and the Right constructor is used to hold a correct value (mnemonic: "right" also means "correct").*

I am going to use the language-ext library in this chapter. It describes this type by saying this:

> *Either monads support either a L (left) or a R (right) value. L is tradition-ally used as an error carrier, and any Either monad carrying an L will short-cut any bind operations and return the L (like an Exception). However, they're not only for that, and can be used to carry an alternative value which could be mapped using BiMap, or MapLeft.*

Note   You can use `Either` to handle any kind of error such as data gathering (for example, missing file or registry key), data validations (for example, invalid password or invalid email address), or severe outage (for example, network unavailability). At the time of this writing, there are three different forms of `Either` in the language-ext library. In this chapter, I'll use the default form, `Either<L, R>`, that does not allow null in its L or R cases.

These definitions essentially highlight the following points:

- The `Either` type helps you describe two possible outcomes.

- There are essentially two values: left and right. The left value indicates that you encountered an error, and the right value indicates that "everything is right."

How Does It Work?

Let's look at some examples to understand how the `Either` type in the language-ext library works. In all these examples, you'll see me invoking the following function that accepts an `Either` instance:

```
void PrintResult(Either<string,int> either)
{
    either.Match
    (
      Left: WriteLine,
      Right: WriteLine
    );
}
```

Note   Example 5 shows the standard practice where `Left` is used to indicate the failure detail and `Right` is used to indicate the output in the happy path.

Note the following:

- In examples 1 to 4, I'll use a function called Test1 that returns an Either type.

- In example 5, I'll use a function called Test2 that accepts Either as an input argument.

- In the final examples, I'll explicitly create two instances of the Either type with left and right states, respectively.

These examples will show how to create and consume instances of the Either type in an application. Do not forget to add the following lines at the top of your .cs file before you test the examples:

```
using LanguageExt;
using static System.Console;
```

Example 1:

The following code uses a function that accepts two integers. Let's assume that this function will show you three different error messages for the following reasons:

- The first argument is negative.

- The second argument is zero.

- The second argument exceeds 100.

If there is no error, the function will return the sum of the integers. Let's investigate the following code and analyze the output:

```
WriteLine("\nTesting Test1(-2, 7)");
Either<string, int> temp = Test1(-2, 7);
PrintResult();
WriteLine(temp.IsLeft);
WriteLine(temp.IsRight);
static Either<string, int> Test1(int a, int b)
{
    if (a < 0) return $"Error: the first argument {a} is
     negative";
    if(b==0) return $"Error: The second argument is {b}";
    if (b>100) return $"Error: {b} exceeds 100";
```

```
    // Everything is OK; returning the sum
    return a+b;
}
```

The following is the output. Notice that this time the `temp` variable is in the left state (i.e., `temp.IsLeft` is True).

```
Testing Test1(-2, 7)
Error: the first argument -2 is negative
True
False
```

You can also see that the returned value is lifted into an `Either` type.

Example 2:

If you replace `Test1(-2,7)` with `Test1(1,0)` in example 1, you will see the following output. Notice that this time the `temp` variable is in the left state (i.e., `temp.IsLeft` is True).

```
Testing Test1(1,0)
Error: The second argument is 0
True
False
```

Example 3:

If you replace `Test1(-2,7)` with `Test1(7, 101)` in example 1, you'll see the following output. Notice that this time the `temp` variable is again in the left state (i.e., `temp.IsLeft` is True).

```
Testing Test1(7, 101)
Error: 101 exceeds 100
True
False
```

Example 4:

If you replace `Test1(-2,7)` with `Test1(6,9)` in example 1, you'll see the following output. In this case, the function did not encounter any error. Notice that this time the `temp` variable is in the right state; i.e., `temp.IsRight` is True.

```
Testing Test1(6, 9)
15
False
True
```

Note   You can think of Either as a fork. Notice that these examples show whenever the "if condition" is satisfied, you reach a dead end and isLeft becomes true. You may also note that a C# implicit conversion is happening here to convert the value (that is either an int or a string) into Either<string, int>.

Example 5:

Given the following code:

```
using static System.Console;
static void Test2(Either<string, int> val)
{
  val.Match
   (
    Right: x => WriteLine($"Correct value: {x}"),
    Left: x => WriteLine($"Incorrect value: '{x}'")
   );
}
```

Test2("Hello") will print Incorrect value: 'Hello'.
Test2(5) will print Correct value: 5.

Example 6:

Now let's test the following code where I reuse the temp variable to create an Either with the left state:

```
// Creating an Either in the Left state
temp = Either<string, int>.Left("This is an error");
WriteLine(temp);
PrintResult();
```

This code generates the following output:

```
Left(this is an error)
This is an error
```

Example 7:

Now let's test the following code where I reuse the temp variable to create an Either with the right state.

```
// Creating an Either in the right state
temp = Either<string, int>.Right(123);
WriteLine(temp);
PrintResult();
```

This code generates the following output:

```
Right(123)
123
```

Handling a Single Exception

You now understand how to use the Either type. In Demonstration 1, you saw how to handle an exception. Let's refactor the code using the Either type. In Demonstration 1, the Calculator function has the int return type. But this time you'll see the Either<Exception,int> return type. Anyone who sees this return type can predict that this function can either raise an exception or produce the intended result that has the return type double. You have already seen that, in either case, the returned value is lifted into an Either.

Demonstration 2

Here is the complete program:

```
using LanguageExt;
using static System.Console;

WriteLine("***Demonstration 2: exception handling in FP.***");

int dividend = new Random().Next(10, 12);
int divisor = new Random().Next(3);
```

```
WriteLine($"Dividend: {dividend}, Divisor: {divisor}");
var result = Calculator.GetQuotient(dividend, divisor);

result.Match(
    Right: success => WriteLine($"Quotient={success}"),
    Left: error => WriteLine($"Error: {error}")
    );

class Calculator
{
    public static Either<Exception, int> GetQuotient(int a,
     int b)
    {
        return b == 0
        ? new DivideByZeroException("Divisor becomes Zero.")
         : (a / b);
    }
}
```

Output

Here is some sample output (there is no exception):

```
***Demonstration 2: exception handling in FP.***
Dividend: 10, Divisor: 1
Quotient=10
```

Here is another output (with the exception):

```
***Demonstration 2: exception handling in FP.***
Dividend: 11, Divisor: 0
Error: System.DivideByZeroException: Divisor becomes Zero.
```

Q&A Session

8.1 In the previous demonstration, you worked with a function that could fail for only one reason: when the divisor becomes zero. But a function can fail due to various reasons. How can I use it in those contexts?

If you understood the working mechanism of the Either type, it should not be a problem for you. In fact, while describing the examples, I used the Test1 function, which could fail for three different reasons. You can replicate the idea while using the Exception class in your code. You know that the Exception class has many subclasses, and you can use those subclasses per your needs. But at the same time, you should note that I am not encouraging you to create lots of Exception subclasses. Usually, string messages and enums are great approaches to display errors. From Demonstration 3 you will get the idea.

Handling Multiple Exceptions

Let's suppose you want to evaluate the value of an expression **(a/b)+c** where a, b, and c are integers. Let's generate the numbers a and b randomly but allow the user to provide the value for c. In this case, you cannot compute the value of the expression if either of the following is true:

- The random value of b is 0.

- The user provides an invalid input.

The reason is obvious: violation of these points will generate exceptions. Can you make a sample implementation?

You can solve the problem in different ways. For example, in OOP style, you put the suspected code in the try block and place multiple catch blocks after that. In addition, in this case, you must place the catch blocks in the order that handles the most specific exception to the least specific exception. Optionally, you can use the finally block too. But how can you solve the problem in a functional style? Continue reading.

Demonstration 3

If you understand how Either works, you can easily implement this. Here is a sample program for you:

```
using LanguageExt;
using FunctionalCsharp;
using static System.Console;

int a = new Random().Next(10,15);
int b = new Random().Next(3);
```

```csharp
string? input = IO.GetUserInput();
WriteLine($"a={a},b={b},c={input}");
WriteLine($"Trying to compute:(a / b) + c");

Calculator
  .Calculate(a, b, input)
  .Match(
    Right: x => WriteLine($"Result={x}"),
    Left: e => WriteLine($"{e.Message}")
    );

static class Calculator
{
    /// <summary>
    /// It computes (a/b)+c and handles multiple exceptions
    /// </summary>
    public static Either<Exception, int> Calculate(
     int a, int b, string? input)
    {
     bool flag = int.TryParse(input, out int c);
     return !flag
       ? new FormatException("Invalid input: try an integer.")
       : b == 0
         ? new DivideByZeroException("Divisor becomes Zero.")
         : (a / b) + c;
    }
}
static class IO
{
    public static string? GetUserInput()
    {
        WriteLine("Enter an integer:");
        string? input = ReadLine();
        return input;
    }
}
```

Output

Here is some sample output (there is no error; we got the happy path):

```
Enter an integer:
3
a=14,b=1,c=3
Trying to compute:(a / b) + c
Result=17
```

Here is some more output (handled by DivideByZeroException):

```
Enter an integer:
3
a=11,b=0,c=3
Trying to compute:(a / b) + c
Divisor becomes Zero.
```

Here is some more output (handled by FormatException):

```
Enter an integer:
abc
a=11,b=2,c=abc
Trying to compute:(a / b) + c
Invalid input: try an integer.
```

Analysis

Notice that instead of using the Exception subclasses, I could use the string messages to produce the identical output. Here is a sample implementation:

```
public static Either<string, int> Calculate2(int a, int b,
  string? input)
    {
        bool flag = int.TryParse(input, out int c);
        return !flag
            ? $"Invalid input: try an integer."
            : b == 0
                ? $"Divisor becomes Zero."
```

```
          : (a / b) + c;
    }
```

You can use it as follows:

```
Calculator
.Calculate2(a, b, input)
.Match(
    Right: x => WriteLine($"Result={x}"),
    Left: WriteLine
    );
```

Q&A Session

8.2 I see that you have used the IO class. Was this necessary?

No, but I wanted to explicitly show that I am accepting user input. This is just a convenient method. When you work in the functional programming style, you try to separate the I/O in the best possible way. Overall, this is a good practice. This is why I placed the imperative code inside the Main function. I have not separated other I/O components because I have used similar statements inside Main() in some other programs in this book to show you the output. Those are simple statements, and they do not cause any big problems. Still, if you are worried about them, you can use a function, say Display, as shown in the following code:

```
using static System.Console;
public static class IO
{
 public static void Display(object? msg)
 {
  WriteLine(msg);
 }
}
```

Then replace the WriteLine statements with IO.Display. I'll show you a sample in the upcoming demonstration.

Chaining Exceptions

Consider a company that has many employees with different pay rates. Let's assume that at a certain point in time, management wants to offer some promotions to its employees. Management also ensures that when an employee gets a promotion, the employee will receive a minimum of a 10 percent salary hike. In this case, two functions can be involved.

- One function checks the promotional criteria.

- Another function decides the salary hike.

While programming this model, you see that an employee gets a promotion and hike if everything goes well, but there is no guarantee. The reason is obvious: any of these functions can fail.

Demonstration 4

Let's write a sample program that essentially reflects this. Assume that the company decides to promote those employees whose salary does not exceed $15,000. This is why you will see the following function in the upcoming program:

```
public static Either<Exception, Employee> CheckSalary(Employee
 emp)
{
 // Checking the promotion criteria.
 // Fail, if the current salary is more than $15000
 return emp.Salary > 15000
  ? new Exception($"the current salary exceeds $15000.")
  : emp with { PromotionStatus = "Eligible" };
}
```

In addition, when you promote an employee, the minimum hike should be 10 percent. This is why you will see the following function:

```
public static Either<Exception, Employee> ProposeHike(Employee
 emp)
{
 // Verifying the proposed hike for the employee.
```

```
// Fail, if the proposed hike is less than 10%
return emp.Hike < 10
  ? new Exception($"the proposed hike is {emp.Hike}% which is
    less than 10%.")
  : emp with { PromotionStatus = "Eligible" };
}
```

Note   I have intentionally injected a possible error in the upcoming program where you'll see that to decide the salary hike percentage, I create a random number between 8 and 14 (both inclusive) and pass it to the `ProposeHike` function. As a result, this function can return an exception when the random number is less than 10.

In our example, an employee can get a salary hike only when the employee is eligible for the promotion. So, the function (`Verify`) shown in Figure 8-1 chains the conditions and handles the errors accordingly (highlighted and commented for readability).

```
public static void Verify(Employee emp)
{
    HrManager.CheckSalary(emp).Match(
      Right: (Employee emp) =>
      {
          Display(emp);
          // The CheckSalary function successfully executes;
          // so, evaluating the next function.
          HrManager.ProposeHike(emp).Match(
            Right: (Employee emp) =>
            {
                Display($"He/she is eligible for a promotion. Proposed hike: {emp.Hike}%");
            },
            Left: (Exception e) =>
            {
                Display($"Recheck the hike proposal: {e.Message}");
            }
          );
      },
      Left: (Exception e) =>
      {
          Display($"{emp}Cannot promote the employee: {e.Message}");
      }
    );
}
```

Figure 8-1.   *The Verify function chains the exceptions.*

Let's see the complete program now:

```
using LanguageExt;
using static System.Console;

IO.Display("***Chaining functions that can raise errors.***");

// Creating two employees
Employee emp1 = new(id: "E1", salary: 12000);
Employee emp2 = new(id: "E2", salary: 16000.75);

// Proposing a hike percentage
int proposedHike = new Random().Next(8, 15);

// Verifying the promotion eligibility and proposed hike
IO.Verify(emp1 with { Hike = proposedHike });
IO.Verify(emp2 with { Hike = proposedHike });

record class Employee
{
    public string Id { get; }
    public double Salary { get; }
    public string PromotionStatus { get; init; }
    public int Hike { get; init; }

    public Employee(
      string id,
      double salary,
      int hike = 0,
      string promotionStatus = "yet to verify"
      )
    {
        Id = id;
        Salary = salary;
        Hike = hike;
        PromotionStatus = promotionStatus;
    }
    public override string ToString()
```

```
    {
        return $"{Id}'s current salary is ${Salary}.";
    }
}

static class HrManager
{
    public static Either<Exception, Employee> CheckSalary(
     Employee emp)
    {
        // Checking the promotion criteria.
        // Fail, if the current salary is more than $15000
        return emp.Salary > 15000
          ? new Exception($"the current salary exceeds
             $15000.")
          : emp with { PromotionStatus = "Eligible" };
    }
    public static Either<Exception, Employee> ProposeHike(
     Employee emp)
    {
        // Verifying the proposed hike for the employee.
        // Fail, if the proposed hike is less than 10%
        return emp.Hike < 10
          ? new Exception($"the proposed hike is {emp.Hike}%
             which is less than 10%.")
          : emp with { PromotionStatus = "Eligible" };
    }
}
static class IO
{
    public static void Display(object? msg)
    {
        WriteLine(msg);
    }
```

```
    public static void Verify(Employee emp)
    {
        HrManager.CheckSalary(emp).Match(
         Right: (Employee emp) =>
         {
             Display(emp);
             // The CheckSalary function successfully
             // executes; so, evaluating the next function.
             HrManager.ProposeHike(emp).Match(
               Right: (Employee emp) =>
               {
                   Display($"He/she is eligible for a
                     promotion. Proposed hike: {emp.Hike}%");
               },
               Left: (Exception e) =>
               {
                   Display($"Recheck the hike proposal:
                     {e.Message}");
               }
           );
         },
         Left: (Exception e) =>
         {
             Display($"{emp}Cannot promote the employee:
             {e.Message}");
         }
       );
    }
}
```

Output

In this section I show some sample output. You can see that emp2 will never get a promotion because the salary is greater than $15,000. But emp1 can get a promotion with a salary hike. The important output segments are marked in bold for your reference.

Case 1: The Employee instance emp1 gets a promotion and salary hike.

```
***Chaining functions that can raise errors.***
E1's current salary is $12000
```
He/she is eligible for a promotion. Proposed hike: 12%
```
E2's current salary is $16000.75.
```
Cannot promote the employee: the current salary exceeds $15000.

Case 2: The verification process fails. Though the Employee instance emp1 satisfies the criteria to get a promotion, the proposed hike is below 10 percent.

```
***Chaining functions that can raise errors.***
E1's current salary is $12000
```
Recheck the hike proposal: the proposed hike is 8% which is less than 10%.
```
E2's current salary is 16000.75.
```
Cannot promote the employee: the current salary exceeds $15000.

Demonstration 5

The Verify function in the previous demonstration was used to chain different situations. In this demonstration, we replace that function with the following one:

```
public static void Verify(Employee emp)
{
 HrManager
 .CheckSalary(emp)
 .Bind(HrManager.ProposeHike)
 .Match
 (
 Right: emp => Display($"{emp} He/she is eligible for
   promotion. Proposed hike: {emp.Hike}%"),
  Left: e => Display($"{emp} Request failed. Error
   detail: {e.Message}")
);
}
```

Which form of the Verify function is better? Do you like the form used in Demonstration 4 or Demonstration 5? I think you'll agree that this refactored version is much more readable compared to Demonstration 4.

POINT TO NOTE

The indentation problem of Demonstration 4 has a name. In the programming world, we call it a **pyramid of doom**. You have probably seen this many levels of nested indentation to control access to a function. In OOP, the nesting of if statements are quite common. Demonstration 5 avoids this problem.

I did not show you the complete program to avoid repetition. This is because, as mentioned, you needed to replace the Verify function in Demonstration 4 with this new one. There is no change in the remaining parts.

Output

The output of this program will be almost similar to the previous output you saw. I say "almost" because in this program, you handled all the errors (or, exceptions) inside a common Match block. To verify this, let's see some sample output where I mark the important segments in bold for your easy reference.

Once again, you can see that emp2 will never get the promotion because their salary is greater than $15,000. But emp1 can get the promotion with the salary hike.

Case 1: The Employee instance emp1 gets a promotion and salary hike.

```
***Chaining functions that can raise errors.***
E1's current salary is $12000. He/she is eligible for promotion. Proposed
hike: 13%
E2's current salary is $16000.75. Request failed. Error detail: the current
salary exceeds $15000.
```

Case 2: The verification process fails. Though the Employee instance emp1 satisfies the criteria to get a promotion, the proposed hike is less than 10 percent.

```
***Chaining functions that can raise errors.***
E1's current salary is $12000. Request failed. Error detail: the proposed
hike is 9% which is less than 10%.
```

E2's current salary is $16000.75.**Request failed. Error detail: the current salary exceeds $15000.**

In real-world programming, chaining exceptions (or, functions that can fail) is a common activity. You have seen two demonstrations on this topic.

Q&A Session

8.3 Demonstration 4 and Demonstration 5 show two different approaches for chaining functions that can fail. Which one is your preferred approach?

Whenever possible, I like to use the approach that is shown in Demonstration 5, because by avoiding the pyramid of doom, you make your code more readable. To illustrate, assume that management wants to gift a dinner coupon to an employee who is eligible for a promotion with at least a 12 percent salary hike. So, you introduce the following function:

```
// The following function is added for Q&A 8.3
public static Either<Exception, Employee> IssueDinnerCoupon(
 Employee emp)
{
 // Deciding the dinner coupon eligibility.
 // Fail, if the proposed hike is less than 12%
 return emp.Hike < 12
   ? new Exception($"to get a dinner coupon minimum salary hike
     should be 12 %.")
   : emp;
}
```

Then chain it inside the Verify function as follows (changes are in bold):

```
public static void Verify(Employee emp)
{
 CheckSalary(emp)
 .Bind(GiveHike)
 .Bind(IssueDinnerCoupon)
 .Match
  (
   Right: emp => Display($"{emp}.He/she is eligible for a
    promotion with {emp.Hike}% salary hike and a dinner
```

```
  coupon."),
 Left: e => Display($"Request failed.Error detail:
 {e.Message}")
 );
}
```

You can see that this approach is more readable compared to Demonstration 4. We can summarize the benefits of Demonstration 5 as follows:

- It avoids the pyramid of doom; you avoid the nested indentations.

- You can inject (or receive) behavior using functions (instead of hard-coding the behavior as shown in Demonstration 4).

- The code is easy to maintain.

Handling Null Values

Handling null values is a challenging task, and often they are difficult to find. The developers who did not see the `NullReferenceException` are almost impossible to find. There has been lots of discussions on how to handle nulls in an application, and some well-known techniques have evolved from them. For example, developers who are familiar with design patterns are aware of the Null Object pattern, where you create a special object to avoid checks for null object instances. Specifically, you encapsulate the absence of an object by providing a default behavior that does nothing. Figure 8-2 shows the basic structure of this pattern.

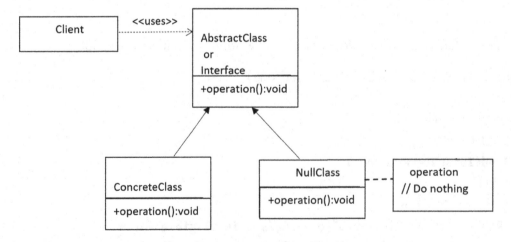

Figure 8-2. *The basic structure of a Null Object pattern*

In C#, you can avoid null checks by using the **null conditional operators**: ?. (for member access) and ?[] (for element access). Still, it can be beneficial for you to learn about the Null Object pattern because, if needed, instead of doing nothing, you can supply a default behavior (that suits your application best) for the null objects. So, before you invoke a member function, checking for nulls is important, and the null conditional operator can help you in that context.

But, you do not necessarily always have to invoke a member function. Instead, you may want to work on the return value of a function. If you are not careful enough, the function can supply you with a null value that can cause typical problems later. So, we cannot ignore the fact that handling nulls is a challenging task. Wikipedia (https:// en.wikipedia.org/wiki/Tony_Hoare#:~:text=Speaking%20at%20a%20software%20 conference,oriented%20language%20(ALGOL%20W)) agrees.

Speaking at a software conference in 2009, Tony Hoare apologized for inventing the null reference.

> *I call it my billion-dollar mistake. It was the invention of the null reference in 1965. At that time, I was designing the first comprehensive type system for references in an object-oriented language (ALGOL W). My goal was to ensure that all use of references should be absolutely safe, with checking performed automatically by the compiler. But I couldn't resist the temptation to put in a null reference, simply because it was so easy to implement. This has led to innumerable errors, vulnerabilities, and system crashes, which have probably caused a billion dollars of pain and damage in the last forty years.*

Since C# allows them, let's investigate how can we handle them functionally.

Introducing the Option Type

Many functional languages do not allow null values at all. For example, read the following (https://wiki.haskell.org/Introduction):

> *Most functional languages, and Haskell in particular, are strongly typed, eliminating a huge class of easy-to-make errors at compile time. In particular, strong typing means no core dumps! There is simply no possibility of treating an integer as a pointer, or following a null pointer.*

What is the alternative? Well, FP likes to use a different type, called `Option`. You can think of it as a container that may or may not contain a value (i.e., the container is empty). As usual, instead of calling it the `Option` type, developers may use a different name. For example, JavaScript and Haskell developers use the name `Maybe` instead of `Option`. I'll stick to the name `Option` or `optional` for the rest of this discussion.

Whatever name you use does not matter much, because the idea is simple: you disallow the possibility of nulls everywhere except the code segment that uses the optional object. This forces you to think about those parts of code that can return a `null`. *It may require changing your coding habits or shifting your mindset to adopt this idea. The key takeaway is that by using optional objects, you ensure that you do not forget about the nulls in specific code segments.* Now the question is, how do you create an optional object? Broadly, you have two choices.

- You can create your own optional object.

- You can use an external library to get the type.

Since I already used language-ext to get the `Either` type, I'll use the same library to get the `Option` type. Obviously, you may choose a different library.

How Does It Work?

Since we are using `LanguageExt` namespace, let's see the documentation to get the optional type (`https://github.com/louthy/language-ext#optional-and-alternative-value-monads`).

> *`Option<T>` works in a very similar way to `Nullable<T>`, except it works with all types rather than just value types. It's a `struct` and therefore can't be null. An instance can be created by either calling `Some(value)`, which represents a positive "I have a value" response, or `None`, which is the equivalent of returning null.*

This link talks about the following types:

- `Option<A>`: This cannot be used with null values.

- `OptionAsync<A>`: This cannot be used with null values with all value realization does asynchronously.

- `OptionUnsafe<T>`: This can be used with null values.

Note   For the discussion in this chapter, understanding the `Option<A>` type will be sufficient for you.

If you understand how to use the `Either` type, understanding the `Option` type is easy. For example, you have seen the following code where you match `Either` with `Right` and `Left`:

```
static void Test2(Either<string, int> val)
{
  val.Match
   (
    Right: x => WriteLine($"Correct value: {x}"),
    Left: x => WriteLine($"Incorrect value: '{x}'")
   );
}
```

In the case of the `Option` type, the possibilities are `Some` and `None`. The `Some` state represents the presence of a valid value, and `None` represents the opposite (the equivalent of returning `null`). To illustrate, here is a sample function that uses the `Option<int>` type:

```
static void Test(Option<int> val)
{
    val.Match
    (
      Some: x => WriteLine($"Received: {x}"),
      None: () => WriteLine($"Did not receive any value.")
    );
}
```

If you investigate this code, you will see that `Option<T>` is a `struct` with many properties and useful methods. Let's go through some examples now. These examples give you the idea of creating and consuming the `Option` type in your application. Do not forget to add the following lines on top of your `.cs` file before you test these examples:

```
using LanguageExt;
using static System.Console;
```

Example 1:

The following code creates three different optional objects, and the Test3 function consumes them. (I explained the Either type examples with functions Test1 and Test2. So, to demonstrate the Option type examples, I have started with the function name: Test3.) To add some flexibility, I am making the Test3 function generic here.

```
Option<int> seven = Option<int>.Some(7);
Option<string> hello = Option<string>.Some("Hello reader!");
Option<int> empty = Option<int>.None;
Test3(seven);
Test3(hello);
Test3(empty);
static void Test3<T>(Option<T> val)
{
    val.Match
      (
      Some: x => WriteLine($"Received: {x}"),
      None: () => WriteLine($"Did not receive any value.")
      );
}
```

If you run this program, it will print the following output:

```
Received: 7
Received: Hello reader!
Did not receive any value.
```

Example 2:

You can also use type inference. For example, by using the var keyword, you can tell the compiler to determine the type of variable. This is why you can replace the following lines in the previous example:

```
Option<int> seven = Option<int>.Some(7);
Option<string> hello = Option<string>.Some("Hello reader!");
Option<int> empty = Option<int>.None;
```

with the following lines to see the same output:

```
var seven = Option<int>.Some(7);
var hello = Option<string>.Some("Hello reader!");
var empty = Option<int>.None;
```

Example 3:

You can further simplify the code. For example, you can replace the following lines:

```
Option<int> seven = Option<int>.Some(7);
Option<string> hello = Option<string>.Some("Hello reader!");
```

with the following lines to see the same output:

```
Option<int> seven = 7;
Option<string> hello = "Hello reader!";
```

Example 4:

Given the following function:

```
static Option<int> Test4()
{
    int random = new Random().Next(2);
    return random > 0 ? random : Option<int>.None;
}
```

you can write something like the following:

```
Test4().Match
(
 Some: x => WriteLine($"Received a positive number: {x}"),
 None: () => WriteLine($"Did not receive any value.")
);
```

Here is some sample output:

```
Received the positive number: 1
```

You can see that the generated random number 1 (which was an `int`) is implicitly converted to `Option<int>`. Similarly, when the random number is 0, this function returns `Option<int>.None`. In other words, in this case, the function implicitly converts to a `None` of `int`. In this case, you'll see the following output:

```
Did not receive any value.
```

POINT TO NOTE

It is important to note that language-ext allows alternative syntaxes as well. For example, you can write the following code (it follows a "fluent" syntax):

```
// Fluent syntax
Test4()
    .Some(x => WriteLine($"Received the positive number: {x}"))
    .None(() => WriteLine($"Did not receive any value."));
```

Remember that our key aim is to understand the usage of the `Option` type. You must follow the syntax that looks more convenient to you. You can learn about the supported format for matching the `Option` type at `https://github.com/louthy/language-ext#option`.

Example 5:

Given the function:

```
static Option<string> Test5(string? input)
{
    return input is not null? input: null;
}
```

the following code:

```
Test5(null)
    .Some(x => WriteLine($"Received: {x}"))
    .None(() => WriteLine($"Got a null value."));
```

will print this:

```
Got a null value.
```

But if you change the return type from Option<string> to OptionUnsafe<string>, it will print the following:

Received:

Why? Per the documentation, OptionUnsafe<T> can be used with null values, but the same does not apply to Option<T> in the LanguageExt namespace.

Example 6:

If you investigate Option<A> in LanguageExt, you will see that Option<A> has a property called Case. Let's use this in the following code segment:

```
Option<int> six = 6;
WriteLine(six.Case);
```

This code will print 6.

Author's note The Either type has a similar property. In FP, instead of using this property, I encourage you to follow the pattern that is shown in the previous examples.

Q&A Session

8.4 How does the **Option** type differ from the **Either** type?

When you use the Either type, you can return any of the two types. For example, Either<Exception, int> indicates that you can return either an Exception or an int type. Since the Exception class has many subclasses, using this type, I could return FormatException and DivideByZeroException as well. Similarly, if you use the type Either<string, int>, you can pass an error message (string type) or an int.

On the other hand, you use the Option type when you are prepared for one particular error such as when the required/expected data is absent. Developers often treat these errors as real defects rather than domain errors. For example, you can search for an employee in a database, but there may be no such employee in the database. So, if you use the Option type, you not only indicate this exceptional situation (when the required data is absent), you define a special behavior as well.

The difference between them will be more prominent if you consider some typical cases when you want some additional information. For example, suppose some students appear in a competitive examination. You understand that all students cannot qualify for this examination. So, in the result board, instead of just marking pass/fail, if you include the details such as their scores and the cutoff marks, a student can get a clearer picture of the performance. I assume that I do not need to tell you that Either is a better choice than Option in this example.

8.5 How does Option<T> differ from Nullable<T>?

The documentation at https://github.com/louthy/language-ext#optional-and-alternative-value-monads, it emphasizes the following points:

- Option<T> works in a similar way to Nullable<T>, except it works with all types rather than just value types.

- Using Option<T>, you explicitly handle both scenarios: the presence or the absence of data. This bulletproofs your code.

- You explicitly tell others that a method may not return a value. This explicit declaration makes the code easy to understand.

Still, you may say that Microsoft (see https://learn.microsoft.com/en-us/dotnet/api/system.nullable-1?view=net-7.0) clearly states the following:

> *The Nullable<T> structure supports using only a value type as a nullable type because reference types are nullable by design.*

If this is the case, let me tell you that, Option<T> has many convenience methods. This makes your programming life easy. If you want, you can write your convenience methods that can sit on top of Nullable types, but as said earlier, using a well-known built-in library makes your code more reliable and can make your programming experience more enjoyable.

Partial Functions and Options

Wikipedia (https://en.wikipedia.org/wiki/Partial_function) says the following:

> *In mathematics, a partial function f from a set X to a set Y is a function from a subset S of X (possibly the whole X itself) to Y. The subset S, that is, the domain of f viewed as a function, is called the domain of definition or natural domain of f. If S equals X, that is, if f is defined on every element in X, then f is said to be a total function.*

In simple words, in the case of a total function, the mapping is defined for every element in the domain. So, following the classical definition of a function, you can say a *total function* is just a function. Since the mapping is defined for every element, given an input, the process of output computation is clear. This is why working with total functions is easy.

On the contrary, in the case of a partial function, mapping is defined for some of the elements, but not for every element in the domain. Following the classical definition of functions, you can say that, by nature, a *partial function* is not even a function. So, working with partial functions may not be straightforward. But in computer science, in many places, we refer to partial functions as simple functions. In many cases, you need to work on partial functions too.

To illustrate, consider the case when you accept a user input (`string`) and try to convert it to an `int`. Let's suppose that someone has written the following function to achieve the task:

```
public int ParseInput(string input)
{
 // Some code
}
```

I do not need to tell you that invalid user inputs cannot be mapped to a valid `int`; so, in this example, `ParseInt` is a partial function. Here you map `string-> int`, but from this method representation, it is not clear how to process the invalid inputs. You may say that in the case of invalid inputs, you'll return some predefined (or, default) value. Yes, that strategy will work, but notice that if you change the return type `int` to `Option<int>`, you make your code clearer and more explicit. In fact, when you map `string->Option<int>`, the `ParseInt` becomes a total function. So, when you need to work on partial functions like this, you can consider refactoring the code using `Option<T>`.

POINT TO NOTE

Microsoft (`https://learn.microsoft.com/en-us/dotnet/standard/linq/refactor-pure-functions`) says that in C#, functions are called *methods*. Throughout this book, I have used *methods* and *functions* interchangeably. Still, I believe that there are some areas where we need to be particular about the terminology. For example, in this chapter, you are seeing the discussions about **partial functions**. In C#, you'll see the presence of **partial methods**. Partial methods allow you to define the method signature in one part of your file and its implementation in another part of the file. If interested, you can learn more about them at https://learn.microsoft.com/en-us/dotnet/csharp/language-reference/ keywords/partial-method. Finally, in Chapter 5, you saw an example of a **partial application** (Q5.3). So, you should not mix and match this terminology.

Q&A Session

8.6 Can you summarize the key benefits of using the `Option` type?

By using the `Option<T>` type, you warn others about the absence of data, and you explicitly handle the scenario. This makes your code clearer and more reliable. Ignoring this contract can cause a compile-time error, but trading the possibility of a compile-time error in exchange for a runtime error such as `NullReferenceException` or `KeyNotFoundException` (when you use the `Dictionary` class) is a better deal.

In addition, when you work with partial functions, using the `Option<T>` type can make your code clearer.

Exercises

E8.1 Can you predict the output of the following program?

```
using LanguageExt;
using static System.Console;

int input = 250;
GetResult(input).Match(
  Left: e => WriteLine($"{e.Message}"),
  Right: WriteLine
);

input = 7250;
GetResult(input).Match(
  Left: e => WriteLine($"{e.Message}"),
  Right: WriteLine
);
static Either<Exception, string> GetResult(int a)
```

```
{
    return a > 5000
        ? new Exception("Please try a number less than 5000.")
        : $"You have entered {a}.";
}
```

E8.2 Can you predict the output of the following program? What will be the output of the program if you set the value **25.5** or **0** for the temp variable in the following program?

```
using LanguageExt;
using static System.Console;

double temp = 250.52;
MakeDouble(temp)
 .Bind(IncrementByFive)
 .Match
  (
   Right: x => WriteLine($"The transformed value is {x}"),
   Left: e => WriteLine($"Error: {e.Message}")
   );

static Either<Exception, double> MakeDouble(double input)
{
    return input <= 0
        ? new Exception($"the number {input} is not positive.")
        : 2 * input;
}

static Either<Exception, double> IncrementByFive(double input)
{
    return input >= 500
      ? new Exception($"the number {input} should be less than
        500")
      : input + 5;
}
```

E8.3 Can you predict the output of the following program?

```
using LanguageExt;
using static System.Console;

Welcome("Kate").Match(
    Some: WriteLine,
    None: () => WriteLine($"Hi Guest! Who are you?")
    );

Welcome(null).Match(
    Some: WriteLine,
    None: () => WriteLine($"Hi Guest! Who are you?")
    );

static Option<string> Welcome(string? input)
{
    return input == null
        ? Option<string>.None
        : $"Hello, {input}! How are you?";
}
```

E8.4 Demonstration 2 shows you how to use the `Either` type. Can you write an equivalent program using the `Option` type?

E8.5 Write a program where a user needs to supply a non-negative integer through the console window. Assume that this program can fail in one of the following ways:

  i)   The user supplies a string that cannot be converted into an `int`.

  ii) The user supplies a negative integer.

  This is why I made the following functions:

```
/// <summary>
/// It parses the user's input
/// </summary>
public static Either<Exception,int> ParseInput(string input)
{
  bool flag = int.TryParse(input, out int initialNumber);
  return !flag
```

```
    ? new FormatException("Invalid input: Try an integer.")
    : initialNumber;
}

/// <summary>
/// It checks whether the integer is positive
/// </summary>
public static Either<Exception,int> CheckNonNegativity (int input)
{
  return input < 0
    ? new Exception("Invalid input: Try an non-negative
     integer.")
    : input;
}
```

Can you write a program that can chain these exceptional situations as well as display valid input?

Summary

This chapter started with a quick recap of exception handling in the OOP style. Then it described some alternative FP-based approaches to deal with exceptional situations or error conditions. In FP, you can handle errors in different ways. This chapter discussed the use of two different types, called Either and Option, that are available in the language-ext library. In brief, it answered the following questions:

- How can you handle a single exception?

- How can you handle multiple exceptions?

- How can you chain exceptions in different ways?

- What kind of challenges may you face that are associated with nulls?

- How can you handle the absence of data (or null)?

Solutions to Exercises

Here are the solutions for the exercises in this chapter.

E8.1

This program produces the following output:

```
You have entered 250.
Please try a number below 5000.
```

Author's note: The lines `Right: x => WriteLine(x)` and `Right: WriteLine` are equivalent.

E8.2

This program produces the following output:

```
Error: the number 501.04 should be less than 500
```

[Clue: `250.52*2= 501.04`]

If `temp=25.5`, you'll see the following output:

```
The transformed value is 56
```

If `temp=0`, you'll see the following output:

```
Error: the number 0 is not positive.
```

E8.3

This program produces the following output:

```
Hello, Kate! How are you?
Hi Guest! Who are you?
```

E8.4

Here is a sample program:

```
using LanguageExt;
using static System.Console;

int dividend = new Random().Next(10, 12);
int divisor = new Random().Next(3);
WriteLine($"Dividend: {dividend}, Divisor: {divisor}");
var value4 =
GetQuotient(dividend, divisor)
 .Match
  (
   Some: x => WriteLine($"{dividend}/{divisor}= {x}"),
   None: () => WriteLine("Error: Divisor becomes Zero.")
  );
static Option<int> GetQuotient(int a, int b)
{
    return b != 0
        ? a / b
        : Option<int>.None;
}
```

Output

Here is some sample output (the divisor is not 0):

```
Dividend: 11, Divisor: 2
11/2= 5
```

Here is some more output (the divisor is 0):

```
Dividend: 11, Divisor: 0
Error: Divisor becomes Zero.
```

E8.5

```csharp
using LanguageExt;
using static System.Console;
using static Calculator;
using static IO;

var input = GetUserInput();
Validate(input);

static class Calculator
{
 /// <summary>
 /// It parses the user's input
 /// </summary>
 public static Either<Exception, int> ParseInput(string input)
 {
   bool flag = int.TryParse(input, out int number);
   return !flag
    ? new FormatException("Invalid input: Try an integer.")
    : number;
  }

 /// <summary>
 /// It checks whether the integer is positive
 /// </summary>
 public static Either<Exception, int> CheckNonNegativity(int input)
 {
  return input < 0
   ? new Exception("Invalid input: Try an non-negative integer.")
   : input;
 }
}

static class IO
{
    public static string? GetUserInput()
    {
```

```
    WriteLine("Enter a non-negative integer:");
    string? input = ReadLine();
    return input;
}
public static void Validate(string input)
{
    // Using in-built Bind function from LanguageExt
    ParseInput(input)
     .Bind(CheckNonNegativity)
     .Match(
     Right: x => WriteLine($"Great. Entered a valid number: {x}"),
     Left: (e) => WriteLine($"Error: {e.Message}")
     );
}
}
```

Output

Here is some sample output for you.

Case 1: The ParseInput function failed.

```
Enter a non-negative integer:
hi
Error: Invalid input: Try an integer.
```

Case 2: The CheckNonNegativity function failed.

```
Enter a non-negative integer:
-25
Error: Invalid input: Try a non-negative integer.
```

Case 3: Control passes through the happy path.

```
Enter a non-negative integer:
37
Great. Entered a valid number: 37
```

CHAPTER 9

Miscellaneous Topics

Welcome to the final chapter of this book! You have seen many functional programming (FP) concepts and how they fit into C# development. Undoubtedly, FP is a big topic, and there is more to learn. In the previous chapters, I aimed to cover some of the essential aspects of FP so that you can harness the concepts and make better programs. I believe that I have achieved this goal.

Then why do we have this chapter? I want to summarize any topics that I might have missed in the previous chapters. In addition, some of these topics could not be discussed in a previous chapter, because they are interlinked. Let's explore those topics.

Helpful Features for FP

We cannot ignore the fact that C# is primarily an object-oriented programming (OOP) language. The previous chapters of the book showed you that C# supports FP as well. In this section, we'll quickly recap some useful features (and concepts) that can help you in FP.

Delegates and Lambdas

In C#, delegates and lambda expressions are the heart of FP. As such, I have used the built-in delegates (`Func` and `Action`) and lambda expressions in many examples and exercises in this book. Particularly, in Chapter 1 and Chapter 2, you saw them when I discussed functions as first-class citizens and higher-order functions (HOFs). These concepts are essential for functional programming.

© Vaskaran Sarcar 2023
V. Sarcar, *Introducing Functional Programming Using C#*, https://doi.org/10.1007/978-1-4842-9697-4_9

Anonymous Methods

The concept of anonymous functions was introduced in C# 2.0 with anonymous delegates, but I did not use them. Why? There is a better alternative, called lambda expressions. These were introduced in C# 3.0, and you can use them to create anonymous functions. Because of their concise syntax, lambda expressions became more popular than anonymous delegates. To illustrate, the following program uses an anonymous delegate as well as a lambda expression (I have marked the important segments in bold):

```
using static System.Console;

const int a = 1, b = 2;
// Using anonymous delegate (C# 2.0 onwards)
WriteLine("Using an anonymous delegate:");
Func<int,int,int> result1= delegate (int x, int y) { return x + y; };
WriteLine($"{a}+{b}= {result1(a,b)}");

// Using a lambda expression(C# 3.0 onwards)
WriteLine("Using a lambda expression:");
Func<int, int, int> result2 = (x, y) => x + y;
WriteLine($"{a}+{b}= {result2(a, b)}");
```

When you run this program, you will see the following output:

```
Using an anonymous delegate:
1+2= 3
Using a lambda expression:
1+2= 3
```

You can see that each of these segments produces the same output, but the lambda expression provides a more concise as well as expressive code compared to the anonymous delegate.

On the contrary, using the delegate operator, you can omit the parameter list and write something like the following:

```
Action sayHello = delegate { WriteLine("Hello, reader!"); };
sayHello();
```

This code can produce the following output as well:

```
Hello, reader!
```

Similarly, the following code:

```
Action <string,int> sayWelcome = delegate { WriteLine("Welcome, reader!"); };
sayWelcome("abc",7);
```

produces the output:

```
Welcome, reader!
```

You can see that anonymous method can be converted to a delegate type with any list of parameter. Microsoft (https://learn.microsoft.com/en-us/dotnet/csharp/language-reference/operators/delegate-operator) says the following:

> *That's the only functionality of anonymous methods that isn't supported by lambda expressions. In all other cases, a lambda expression is a preferred way to write inline code.*

Extension Methods and LINQ

In addition to delegates and lambda expressions, I have used the extension methods throughout this book. They are very useful in FP.

Ask any C# developer about LINQ. The first thing you will probably hear is that it is a functional API in C#. When I discussed the built-in HOFs, I showed you the signature of the Where function, which is an extension method. The same is true for the Select function as well.

In Chapter 7, you learned that LINQ users choose either query syntax or method syntax. I chose to use the method syntax and explained the reason behind this choice. If you like query syntax, you will use select instead of Select, where instead of Where, and so on. Here is some code sample that shows both approaches:

```
List<string> names = new() { "Sam", "Jo","Bob" };
// Using the method syntax
var query2 = names
            .Where(name => name.Length > 2)
            .Select(name=>name);
```

```
// Using the query Syntax
var query1 = from name in names
            where name.Length > 2
            select name;
```

On further analysis, you will see that it does not matter whether you use the select query or the Select function; in both cases, you are using an extension method.

At the same time, their uses are not limited to FP. Microsoft nicely summarizes their importance by saying the following (see https://learn.microsoft.com/en-us/dotnet/csharp/programming-guide/classes-and-structs/extension-methods):

> *For those occasions when the original source isn't under your control, when a derived object is inappropriate or impossible, or when the functionality shouldn't be exposed beyond its applicable scope, Extension methods are an excellent choice.*

This is why you will be tempted to use extension methods on many occasions. But you must remember the following points before you use them:

- If an extension method has the same signature as the method defined in the type (for which you add this method), it will never be invoked.

- The extension methods are brought into scope with the using directive. But if you have multiple static classes with extension methods in a single namespace, they will all be brought into scope when you use the using directive. This means you may bring some unnecessary methods in the scope, and as a result, those methods can be misused by others.

- Microsoft also warns you (see the previous link) by saying the following:

> *For a class library that you implemented, you shouldn't use extension methods to avoid incrementing the version number of an assembly.*

C# extension methods are really useful compiler syntax sugar. For example, when using the LINQ extension method in numbers.Where(predicate), the code that really compiles is Enumerable.Where(numbers, predicate).

It is also important to note that at the CLR level, something similar happens: all C# instance methods are called like static methods in CLR receiving the `this` instance as a parameter. For example, at the CLR level, `someObject.Method(a, b)` is converted into `Method(someObject, a, b)`. This is an example of how hidden parameter complexity can make function usage more natural and friendly.

Q&A Session

9.1 You said that `someObject.Method(a, b)` is converted into `Method(someObject, a, b)`. How can I verify this?

ECMA-335 (5th edition) says the following:

> *A method that is associated with an instance of the type is either an instance method or a virtual method. When they are invoked, instance and virtual methods are passed the instance on which this invocation is to operate (known as* this *or a* this *pointer).*

> *The fundamental difference between an instance method and a virtual method is in how the implementation is located. An instance method is invoked by specifying a class and the instance method within that class. Except in the case of instance methods of generic types, the object passed as* this *can be null (a special value indicating that no instance is being specified) or an instance of any type that inherits from the class that defines the method.*

You can also verify this if you write a simple program, compile it, and verify the IL code. For example, consider the following program:

```
using static System.Console;

Person.StaticMethod();

Person person = new();
person.InstanceMethod();
class Person
{
    public void InstanceMethod()
    {
        WriteLine("Invoked InstanceMethod().");
    }
}
```

261

```
    public static void StaticMethod()
    {
        WriteLine("Invoked StaticMethod().");
    }

}
```

See the IL code as shown in Figure 9-1.

```
 Program::<Main>$ : void(string[])                                    —    □    ×

Find   Find Next
.method private hidebysig static void  '<Main>$'(string[] args) cil managed
{
    .entrypoint
    // Code size        20 (0x14)
    .maxstack  1
    .locals init (class Person V_0)
    IL_0000:  call        void Person::StaticMethod()
    IL_0005:  nop
    IL_0006:  newobj      instance void Person::.ctor()
    IL_000b:  stloc.0
    IL_000c:  ldloc.0
    IL_000d:  callvirt    instance void Person::InstanceMethod()
    IL_0012:  nop
    IL_0013:  ret
} // end of method Program::'<Main>$'
```

Figure 9-1. *IL code*

Notice that the `callvirt` instruction is used for the instance method, whereas the `call` instruction is used for the static method. What does `callvirt` do? See the documentation at `https://learn.microsoft.com/en-us/dotnet/api/system.reflection.emit.opcodes.callvirt?view=net-7.0`. You can see the following information:

- The `callvirt` instruction calls a late-bound method on an object. That is, the method is chosen based on the runtime type of `obj` rather than the compile-time class visible in the method pointer. `callvirt` can be used to call both virtual and instance methods.

- The `callvirt` pops the object and the associated arguments off the evaluation stack before calling the method. If the method has a return value, it is pushed on the stack upon method completion. **On the callee side, the `obj` parameter is accessed as argument 0, `arg1` as argument 1, and so on.**

Note   To see the IL code, you can open the Developer's Command Prompt for VS, type `ildasm`, and press Enter. the ILDASM window will open and you can drag the `dll` into it.

Type Inference

Type inference is often treated as an FP feature rather than an OOP feature. Have you noticed the use of the `var` keyword and `new()` expressions in different code segments in this book? For example, in Chapter 1, you saw the following line:

```
List<string> names = new() { "Sam", "Bob" };
```

instead of this:

```
List<string> names = new List<string>(){ "Sam", "Bob" };
```

In Chapter 8, I used the following:

```
var seven = Option<int>.Some(7);
```

instead of this:

```
Option<int> seven = Option<int>.Some(7);
```

You can see that these features help the compiler infer the proper types. Implicitly typed local variables (`var` keyword) were introduced in C# 3, and target-typed new expressions were introduced in C# 9.

Importing Static Members

Throughout this book, you have seen me using the following line:

```
using static System.Console;
```

You have seen similar statements in other code segments too. For example, in Exercise 8.5, you saw the following lines:

```
using static Calculator;
using static IO;
```

This kind of statement allowed me to import the `static` members of the class. Using this facility, I could avoid further qualifications. For example, I could write something like the following:

```
WriteLine("Some message.");
```

instead of this:

```
Console.WriteLine("Some message.");
```

From C# 10 onward, you can add the `global` modifier to a using directive to indicate that `using` is applied to all files in a project. Here is a sample for you:

```
 global using static System.Math;
```

Q&A Session

9.2 I understand that importing static members can avoid having to use further qualifications. But how can it help in FP?

FP relies on pure functions so that you can test them in isolation. Usually, these functions are implemented as static methods in a C# functional library. The `using` `static` statements can help you consume those libraries easily.

Immutability Features

You saw a detailed discussion on immutability in Chapter 3. There you learned about different kinds of immutability such as external immutability, internal immutability, shallow immutability, and popsicle immutability. I started the discussion with private setters and read-only properties. You saw that you could assign the values for the read-only properties inside the constructors only. This feature promotes immutability.

Later, I continued the discussion with useful features such as the `record` type, `with` `expression`, and `init` accessor, which have been available since C# 9.0. In addition, if you want to work with an immutable structure, you can have `readonly struct` types too (C# 7.2 onward).

Expression-Bodied Members

Consider the following program:

```
using static System.Console;
Employee emp = new("Kevin", "Smith");
WriteLine($"Employee name: {emp.FullName()}");

class Employee
{
    public string FirstName { get; }
    public string LastName { get; }
    public Employee(string firstName, string lastName)
    {
        FirstName= firstName;
        LastName= lastName;
    }
    public string FullName()
    {
        return $"{FirstName} {LastName}";
    }

}
```

There is no magic here; when executing this program, you can see the following output:

```
Employee name: Kevin Smith
```

But you can write a concise code using expression body definitions. An expression body definition has the following syntax:

```
member=> SomeValidExpression
```

For example, you can replace the FullName() method in the previous code using the following:

```
public string FullName => $"{FirstName} {LastName}";
```

Notice that similar to a lambda expression, the return keyword is not used here. So, now you can refactor the previous program as follows (notice the changes in bold):

```
using static System.Console;
Employee emp = new("Kevin", "Smith");
WriteLine($"Employee name: {emp.FullName()}");

class Employee
{
    public string FirstName { get; }
    public string LastName { get; }
    public Employee(string firstName, string lastName)
    {
        FirstName= firstName;
        LastName= lastName;
    }
    public string FullName() => $"{FirstName} {LastName}";
}
```

POINT TO NOTE

Throughout in Chapter 3, you have seen me using the ToString() method in this form:

```
public override string ToString() =>  $"Name: {Name}, ID: {Id}";
```

Lastly, I have shown you how to use an expression-bodied method. In addition, C# supports expression-bodied properties and constructors. Here is a typical sample for your reference (I have marked important changes in bold):

```
class Employee
{
    public string FirstName { get; }
    public string? LastName { get; }
    public Employee(string firstName) =>
        FirstName = firstName;
```

```
    public Employee(string firstName, string lastName)
    {
        FirstName = firstName;
        LastName = lastName;
    }
    public string FullName => $"{FirstName} {LastName}";

}
```

Remember that in the case of an expression-bodied constructor, Microsoft (see https://learn.microsoft.com/en-us/dotnet/csharp/programming-guide/ statements-expressions-operators/expression-bodied-members) says the following:

> *An expression body definition for a constructor typically consists of a single assignment expression or a method call that handles the constructor's arguments or initializes instance state.*

This is why you may notice that lastName was not used in the expression-bodied constructor. If you write something like the following:

```
// Invalid code
public Employee(string firstName, string lastname) =>
{
    FirstName = firstName;
    LastName=lastName;
}
```

you will see compile-time errors.

How can you use an expression-bodied constructor if you need to use multiple parameters? The answer is that you can use a one-liner method invocation that sets the arguments. But it is not a recommended approach. Here is a sample:

```
// Not a recommended approach
public Employee(string firstName, string lastname) =>
 SetName(firstName, lastname);

void SetName(string firstName, string lastName)
{
 FirstName = firstName;
 LastName = lastName;
}
```

267

Instead, you can use tuple deconstruction as follows:

Here is a sample solution (notice the important changes in bold):

```
class Employee
{
    public string FirstName { get; set; }
    public string LastName { get; set; }

    // Better approach
    public Employee(string firstName, string lastname) =>
      (FirstName, LastName) = (firstName, lastname);

    public string FullName => $"{FirstName} {LastName}";
}
```

Q&A Session

9.3 How do the expression-bodied members help me in FP?

FP uses many simple functions that are just one-liners. Later, you compose those functions. Expression-bodied members help you write those simple functions in a concise and readable form.

Local Functions

C# allows you to define a function inside another function. Before we discuss the associated benefits, let's see the following code that contains two local functions, MakeDouble and MakeSquare:

```
class Circle
{
    public Circle(double radius)
    {
        Radius = radius;
    }
    public double Radius { get; }
```

```
public double GetCircumference()
{
  static double MakeDouble(double value) => 2 * value;
  return 3.14* MakeDouble(Radius);
}

public double GetArea()
{
  static double MakeSquare(double value) => value * value;
  return 3.14 * MakeSquare(Radius);
}
}
```

This is a contrived example, but it shows the use of local functions perfectly.

Q&A Session

9.4   How do local functions help me in FP?

FP uses lots of simple functions, and local functions are just simple functions. You can refactor a complex function by segregating the business logic into these local functions to improve code readability.

You'll also probably agree that to understand complex code, a named function is often a better choice than an unnamed function.

What happens if you extract a function from another function but do not make it local? After the call/usage, it may become an orphan and hang around the API. So, it is better to use local functions instead of making those orphan functions.

In addition, Microsoft (`https://learn.microsoft.com/en-us/dotnet/csharp/programming-guide/classes-and-structs/local-functions`) states the following:

> *Local functions make the intent of your code clear. Anyone reading your code can see that the method is not callable except by the containing method. For team projects, they also make it impossible for another developer to mistakenly call the method directly from elsewhere in the class or struct.*

Tuples

C# allows you to create and consume tuples easily. Starting from C# 7, using tuples has become easier. Using tuples, you can group multiple data elements into a simple data structure. For example, see the following code (I have used raw-string literals, a C# 11 feature, in this code segment for better alignment):

```
(int,double,string) tuple = (3,7.5, "hello");
WriteLine($"""
 1st element: {tuple.Item1}
 2nd element: {tuple.Item2}
 3rd element: {tuple.Item3}
 """);
```

This code will produce the following output:

```
1st element: 3
2nd element: 7.5
3rd element: hello
```

As usual, you can use the `var` keyword instead of explicitly mentioning the type of the tuple elements as `(int,double,string)`.

The problem is that this type of syntax is inconvenient if you have multiple elements with similar data types. With the introduction of `ValueTuple` in C#, this problem is solved. Now, you can write something like the following:

```
(string fName, string lName) fullName= ("Sumit", "Jain");
WriteLine($"First name: {fullName.fName} Last name:
 {fullName.lName}");
```

Obviously, this code reduces the complexity, and it is more readable.

Let's analyze another use case of `ValueTuple`. The following code (see the `GetDetails` function inside the `Circle` type) demonstrates a typical use case where you return multiple values from a function:

```
class Circle
{
    static internal (double perimeter,double area) GetDetails(double radius)
    {
```

```
        return (2 * 3.14 * radius, 3.14 * radius * radius);
    }
}
```

Instead of using a method, you can also use a property with a meaningful name to improve code readability. Here is a sample for you (see the Details property):

```
class Circle2
{
    public double Radius { get; set; }
    public (double Circumference, double Area) Details =>
    (2 * 3.14 * Radius, 3.14 * Radius * Radius);
}
```

Tuples are a big topic, and I suggest that you learn more about them.

Q&A Session

9.5 What are the benefits of using tuples?

In short, tuples provide the following benefits:

- You can return multiple values from a function without using the out parameters.

- You can pass multiple values to a function through a single parameter.

- You can hold some values temporarily without creating a dedicated type. This point is important because FP uses many small functions. You may need to hold the return values of those functions temporarily before you pass them to a different function.

9.6 In some technical discussions, developers sometimes say that tuples are value types. In other discussions, they say that tuples are reference types. I am confused. Can you throw some light on this?

You are probably confused about ValueTuple and Tuple in C#. You have already seen that the newly introduced ValueTuple (which is a struct) allows you to use meaningful element names, which is not possible with old Tuple class. In addition, there are some important distinctions between them. Microsoft (see https://learn.microsoft. com/en-us/dotnet/csharp/language-reference/builtin-types/value-tuples) summarizes the points as follows:

C# tuples, which are backed by System.ValueTuple types, are different from tuples that are represented by System.Tuple types. The main differences are as follows:

- System.ValueTuple types are value types. System.Tuple types are reference types.

- System.ValueTuple types are mutable. System.Tuple types are immutable.

- Data members of System.ValueTuple types are fields. Data members of System.Tuple types are properties.

Pattern Matching

Pattern matching helps you test an expression to determine whether it fulfills certain characteristics. FP likes to use the technique often in different scenarios. Here I include some examples.

Example 1:

In Chapter 8 I used the following code:

```
static Option<string> Test5(string? input)
{
    return input is not null? input: null;
}
```

Here I used the "not" pattern to check the null input.

Example 2:

Consider the following program, which tries to convert a nullable value type to its underlying type:

```
using static System.Console;
int? maybe = 25;
string testResult= maybe is int value ?
    $"The 'maybe' holds the value: {value}" :
    "The nullable int 'maybe' doesn't hold a value";
WriteLine(testResult);
```

Once you run this program, you will see the following output:

```
The 'maybe' holds the value: 25
```

Example 2 also checks for the null values. Both example 1 and example 2 represent common scenarios for pattern matching.

Example 3:

Consider the following program. This example tests whether the variables person1 and emp1 match a given type (Employee).

```
using static System.Console;
Person person1 = new() { Name = "John" };
Person person2 = new Employee { Name = "Bob", ID = 1 };

var result1 = person1 is Employee e1
    ? $"{e1}"
    : $"{person1} is not an employee";
WriteLine(result1);
var result2 = person2 is Employee e2
    ? $"{e2}"
    : $"{person2} is not an employee";
WriteLine(result2);

class Person
{
    public string Name { get; set; }
    public override string ToString() => $"{Name}";

}
class Employee:Person
{
    public int ID { get; set; }
    public override string ToString() =>
     $"{Name} is an employee with ID: {ID}";
}
```

Once you run this program, you will see the following output:

```
John is not an employee
Bob is an employee with ID: 1
```

Example 4:

Example 3 can be simplified using the switch expression. For example, you get the same output if you replace the following code segment:

```
var result1 = person1 is Employee e1
    ? $"{e1}"
    : $"{person1} is not an employee";
WriteLine(result1);
var result2 = person2 is Employee e2
    ? $"{e2}"
    : $"{person2} is not an employee";
WriteLine(result2);
```

with the following one that uses the switch expression:

```
var result3=CheckPattern(person1);
WriteLine(result3);
var result4=CheckPattern(person2);
WriteLine(result4);
// Switch expression
string CheckPattern(Person p) => p switch
{
    Employee e => $"{e}",
    _ => $"{p} is not an employee"
};
```

In addition to these tests, you can compare discrete values, test relational patterns, list patterns (a C# 11 feature), and so on. I encourage you to read the online documentation at https://learn.microsoft.com/en-us/dotnet/csharp/fundamentals/functional/pattern-matching to learn more about pattern matching.

We have done a quick review of some of the useful C# features that can help you write functional code. Let's move on to the next topic.

Revisiting Option<T>

I discussed the Bind pattern in Chapter 7 and the Option<T> type in Chapter 8. Each of these chapters was big. Here, I will discuss the Bind pattern with Option<T> before I discuss monads.

Please complete Exercise 8.5 in the previous chapter before you read further. There you apply the Bind pattern on two methods that have return type <Exception,int>. Now we'll work with Option<T>. So, let's make the necessary changes as follows (see the key changes in bold):

```
/// <summary>
/// It validates the user's input
/// </summary>
public static Option<int> ParseInput(string input)
{
  bool flag = int.TryParse(input, out int initialNumber);
   return !flag
       ? Option<int>.None
       : initialNumber;
}

/// <summary>
/// It checks whether the integer is positive
/// </summary>
public static Option<int> CheckNonNegativity(int input)
{
  return input < 0
    ? Option<int>.None
    : input;
}
```

Let me ask you a question: **can you write a program that can chain these methods so that you can handle exceptional situations as well as display that valid input?** You saw that the Either type has a Bind method. Option<T> also has a method with the same name, and you can use it here. But before I use that built-in method, let's try to solve the problem with our custom method. This can help you understand (and, review) the concept of the Bind pattern.

QA 7.8 in Chapter 7 showed you a general signature of the Bind pattern, as follows:

Bind: `(C<T>,T->C<R>)->C<R>`

Let's replace C with `Option` to understand the pattern for `Option<T>`.

Bind(for Option<T>): `(Option<T>,T->Option<R>)->Option<R>`

What does this mean? This `Bind` function takes an `Option<T>` and an `Option`-returning function (`Option<R>`) and applies that function to the inner value of `Option<T>`.

In the case of the `Option<T>` type, the possibilities are `Some` and `None`. The `Some` state represents the presence of a valid value, and `None` represents the opposite (the equivalent of returning `null`).

So, I can make the following extension method (`BindWith`):

```csharp
public static Option<int> BindWith(
  this Option<int> container,
  Func<int, Option<int>> f)
{
  return container.Match(
    Some: x => f(x),
    None: () => Option<int>.None);
}
```

Now, the following code can work:

```csharp
var input = GetUserInput(); // Getting a user input
Validate(input);
```

where the `Validate` function is defined as follows:

```csharp
public static void Validate(string input)
{
  ParseInput(input)
  .BindWith(CheckNonNegativity)
  .Match(
  Some: x => WriteLine($"Great.Entered a valid number: {x}"),
  None: () => WriteLine($"You did not entered a positive
            (or, valid)number.")
 );
}
```

Though this can solve the problem, a generic version of the BindWith function can be a better solution. So, let's try the following implementation:

```
// Generic Version
public static Option<R> GenericBindWith<T,R>(
  this Option<T> container,
  Func<T, Option<R>> f)
{

  return container.Match(
    Some: x => f(x),
    None: () => Option<R>.None);
}
```

Now you can replace BindWith with GenericBindWith in the previous segments of the code. This time your program will compile and run.

Bind Function

But if Option<T> has a built-in Bind method, there is no need to use the custom extension method. Let's use the built-in method instead, as shown here:

```
//
// Summary:
// Monad bind operation
[MethodImpl(MethodImplOptions.AggressiveInlining)]
[Pure]
public Option<B> Bind<B>(Func<A, Option<B>> f)
{
  if (!isSome)
  {
   return default(Option<B>);
  }
  return f(Value);
}
```

Author's note You can easily guess that isSome is a Boolean. It is defined as internal readonly bool isSome;.

As usual, there is no surprise that you can replace GenericBindWith function with the language-ext library's built-in function Bind in the previous code as follows:

```
var input = GetUserInput(); // Getting a user input
Validate(input);
```

where the Validate function is defined as follows:

```
public static void Validate(string input)
{
  ParseInput(input)
  .Bind(CheckNonNegativity)
  .Match(
  Some: x => WriteLine($"Great.Entered a valid number: {x}"),
  None: () => WriteLine($"You did not enter a positive
            (or, valid)number.")
 );
}
```

Note   You can download the Demo_BindPatternWithOption project from the Apress website to see the complete program where all three different variations (BindWith, GenericBindWith, and Bind) are used.

You can see that both functions, ParseInput and CheckNonNegativity, have the same return type: Option<int>. Suppose you change the return type of the CheckNonNegativity function from Option<int> to Option<NonNegativeInteger> where the NonNegativeInteger type is defined as follows:

```
public class NonNegativeInteger
{
  public int Number { get; }
  public NonNegativeInteger(int number)
  {
```

```
   // We do not allow any negative number
   Number = number >= 0 ? number : 0;
 }
 public override string ToString()
 {
  return Number.ToString();
 }
}
```

Now I have a question for you: can you chain ParseInt and CheckNonNegativity using the Bind function? I want you to think about it. Otherwise, download the project Demo_BindPatternWithOption2 from the Apress website and see a possible implementation. That program will show you that though ParseInput returns Option<int> and CheckNonNegativity returns Option<NonNegativeInteger>, still you can chain these methods using the Bind function.

Return Function

Now let's test one more code segment, as shown here:

```
using LanguageExt;
using static System.Console;

var option = Option<int>.Some(125);
WriteLine(option);
WriteLine(option.GetType());
```

Can you predict the output? It's easy. You will see the following output:

```
Some(125)
LanguageExt.Option`1[System.Int32]
```

The Some function converts an int to an Option<int>. In other words, this function lifts the normal value 125 to Some(125). The popular functional language Haskell calls this type of function a **Return** function. OOP developers are often confused by this term, because return is always a keyword by default for them. Is there any other standard name for this? Thankfully, yes. This is also known as the **Unit** function. So, you can use the name that you like.

Now we can define a general signature for the Return (or Unit) function as follows:

Return(or, Unit): `T->C<T>`

Introducing Monads

A book on functional programming cannot wrap up without discussing monads. A **monad** is a type that has a Return function as well as a Bind function. You have seen that Option<T> has a Return function. You have seen that Option<T> has a Bind function as well. So, Option<T> is a monad. You have seen Either<L,R> type in the previous chapter. This is another example of a monad.

It can be helpful for an OOP developer to relate to monads with a design pattern. Eric Lippert in his excellent blog post (`https://ericlippert.com/2013/02/25/monads-part-two/#more-464`) says the following:

> The "monad pattern" is a design pattern for types, and a "monad" is a type that uses that pattern.

Definition

For our convenience, let's define monads. A monad is a type C<T> that has the following functions:

Return(Also known as Unit): `T->C<T>`
Bind: `(C<T>,T->C<R>)->C<R>`

Notice that the Return function takes a normal type and lifts (or amplifies) it into a "wrapped" type. The Bind function takes the "wrapped" type and preserves the "amplification."

Later, you'll learn that a proper monad needs to adhere to three fundamental laws (known as **monadic laws**). Haskell heavily uses monads. Let's learn some additional information from it (`https://wiki.haskell.org/All_About_Monads#What_is_a_monad.3F`), as shown here:

> Any type constructor with return and bind operators that satisfy the three monad laws is a monad.

What are these three laws? These monadic laws are often referred to as **left identity**, **right identity**, and **associativity**.

Mathematical Background

Understanding monad laws can be easy if you analyze them from a mathematical background. For example, in mathematics, let (S, ops) be a set S equipped with the binary operation ops. Then an element e of S is called:

- A **left identity** if e ops s = s for all s in S

- A **right identity** if s ops e = s for all s in S

To illustrate, consider the set of positive integers and the addition operation. You can see the following:

```
0+1=1
0+2=2,
0+3=3 and so on.
```

So, **0 is a left identity for positive integers for the addition operation**. Similarly, we have this:

```
1+0=1
2+0=2
3+0=3 and so on.
```

0 is also the right identity for positive integers for the addition operation.

Finally, in the case of **associativity**, rearranging the parentheses in an expression will not change the result. For example, see the following:

```
(1+2)+3=1+(2+3)
```

Monad Laws

How does Haskell define these laws (see https://wiki.haskell.org/Monad_laws)? To be a proper monad, the return and >>= functions must work together according to three laws, as listed here:

Left identity: return a >>= h ≡ h a
Right identity: m >>= return ≡ m
Associativity: (m>>=g)>>= h ≡ m >>= (\x -> g x >>= h)

Here, **p ≡ q** simply means that you can replace p with q, and vice versa, and the behavior of your program will not change: p and q are equivalent.

Understanding the Haskell Notations

If you are seeing these Haskell notions for the first time, it will be difficult to understand these rules. Let me simplify them for you.

- Here >>= denotes the Bind. Similar to the addition operator (+), consider it as a binary operator. The Haskell notion **m>>f** says that you apply a function f to a monadic instance m. It is equivalent to writing m.Bind(f) in C#.

- In Haskell, return is a function that takes an argument and returns a monadic value. To ensure this, see the following function declaration in Haskell:

  ```
  return :: Monad m => a -> m a
  ```

- \x -> f x denotes the anonymous (lambda) function. So, the expression (\x -> f x >>= g) is equivalent to writing this:

  ```
  x=>f(x).Bind(g)
  ```

Monad Laws for C# Developers

Let me represent these monad laws in a better way for C# developers (I like to use f and x instead of h and a while rewriting the monad laws).

- **Return(x).Bind(f) == f(x)**

  This law says that first, applying Return on x and then applying Bind to the function f on that result will be equivalent to directly applying f to x. In other words, **Return is a left identity for Bind**.

- **m.Bind(Return)== m**

  This law says that if you bind the Return function on the monadic value x, you'll get the x. Bind unwraps the value and then applies Return to it. In other words, **Return is also the right identity for Bind**.

- `m.Bind(f).Bind(g)== m.Bind(x=>f(x).Bind(g))`

  Bind is essentially associative. You may be confused: why was the associativity written like this? Ideally, in Haskell notations, it was supposed to be written like the following:

  $$(m >>= f) >>= g \equiv m >>= (f >>= g)$$

But take a close look at the right-hand side of the equation. Bind (`>>=`) expects the left operand to be a monadic value, whereas f is a function but not a monadic value. So, syntactically, `f >>= g` is wrong. But note that f can be expanded in the lambda form, `\x -> f x`, so you can rewrite the right side as follows:

$$m >>= (\backslash x -> f x >>= g)$$

This is why the associativity is represented in the following form:

$$(m >>= f) >>= g \equiv m >>= (\backslash x -> f x >>= g)$$

Now you understand that, in the case of associativity, the following should hold:

`(m.Bind(f)).Bind(g)==  m.(Bind(f).Bind(g))`

On the right side of the equation, replacing f with x=>f(x), we can write this:

`m.(Bind(f).Bind(g)) ==  m.(Bind(x=>f(x)).Bind(g))`

By removing the extra brackets on both sides of the equation, this law can be further simplified as follows:

`m.Bind(f).Bind(g)==m.Bind(x=>f(x).Bind(g))`

Now your job will be testing whether a monad truly satisfies these monadic laws. I leave this exercise to you (if you cannot solve this problem, refer to the solution to problem E9.7).

Chaining Multi-argument Functions

See the right-hand side of the associativity. I expanded f to its lambda form. This time, expand g too. So, **`m.Bind(x=>f(x).Bind(g))`** becomes the following:

`m.Bind(x=>f(x).Bind(y=>g(y)))`

Notice that g has visibility to both x and y this time. This allows you to handle multi-argument functions as well. For example, in the following program, the square function works with a single argument, and the multiply function works with multiple arguments. Still, I can chain them using the Bind function. Here is the sample program where the intermediate values in each step are shown using comments:

```
using LanguageExt;
using static System.Console;

Func<int, Option<int>> square = x => x * x;
Func<int, int, Option<int>> multiply = (x, y) => x * y;

// Passing multiple arguments
var result = Option<int>.Some(3)  // Some(3)
            .Bind(x => square(x)  // Some(9)
                .Bind(y => multiply(x, y)));    // Some(3*9)
WriteLine(result); // Some(27)
```

Note that you can make the code more readable by using local functions. For example, you can replace the following lines in the previous code segment:

```
Func<int, Option<int>> square = x => x * x;
Func<int, int, Option<int>> multiply = (x, y) => x * y;
```

with the following lines and get the same output:

```
Option<int> square(int x) => x * x;
Option<int> multiply(int x, int y) => x * y;
```

You should now understand the fundamental ideas of monads. Remember that the concept of monads is a big topic. If you're interested in learning more, you can visit the online Haskell wiki page (https://wiki.haskell.org/All_About_Monads#The_three_fundamental_laws). I also recommend the series of blog posts by Eric Lippert (https://ericlippert.com/category/monads/). Enrico Buonanno's book *Functional Programming in C#* is another nice resource.

Final Suggestions

Before I finish this chapter, I'd like to share some personal opinions that are not limited to functional programming. You may take note of them before you start coding for your next real-world application.

Command Query Separation

In Chapter 6, you saw the Functional Core, Imperative Shell pattern. Using this pattern you separated the functional code (business logic) from the imperative code I/O. Remember that separating code based on its nature is a nice idea. For example, you may have heard about *command query separation* (CQS). This term was coined by Bertrand Meyer in his influential book *Object-Oriented Software Construction*. Let's see what commands and queries are.

- *Queries* return a result. These are free of side effects.

- *Commands* change the state of a system but do not return a value.

You can think of these commands as mutators or simply modifiers. Wikipedia (`https://en.wikipedia.org/wiki/Command%E2%80%93query_separation`) explains it.

> *It(CQS) states that every method should either be a command that performs an action, or a query that returns data to the caller, but not both. In other words, asking a question should not change the answer.*

Obviously, there are some exceptions to this rule, but in general, it is a good idea to separate commands from queries! Notice that CQS focuses on methods in OOP. But you know that methods are just functions. So, when you design functions in FP, you can keep this in mind.

Learn Design Patterns and Anti-Patterns

Design patterns help you write better code and understand code written by a professional in a better way. I have written several books on design patterns and sincerely believe that once you master them, you will be more confident about your coding ability. At the same time, you will be able to organize your code better.

Learning design patterns is essential for good programmers. Why? At a very high level, they accelerate your development process. An experienced developer knows how to reduce future effort by simply reusing the concepts already in place. Design patterns address this kind of issue and provide a common platform for all developers. You can think of them as the recorded experience of experts in the field.

It is also essential to learn about anti-patterns. Why? Anti-patterns not only warn about common mistakes but also suggest better solutions. Some of these solutions may not be attractive at the beginning, but in the long run, they save your time, your effort, your reputation.

Don't Let Failures Stop You

I like to learn from great personalities because a lot of advice is universal. One such piece of advice is: no failure is a true failure unless you accept it. As software developers, we are continuously developing new functionalities or features. When the test team validates them, you may see that many of the test cases do not pass. For example, if a test suite contains 100 test cases, the result may show **pass, pass, fail, pass, fail, fail, fail, pass, fail, fail, and so on**. This is quite natural. But I have seen that often people like to see only "passes," but not failures. All you need to do is fix the failures one by one. Often, a fix in one place can fix many problems in other places. In fact, if I do not see any test failures with my initial development, I doubt the strength of the test suite. You should not forget the hard truth: your job is to produce good-quality software, not to produce code that passes every test in a test suite.

See the following quote by Edsger W.Dijkstra, a pioneer in computer science (see `https://www.goodreads.com/quotes/506689-program-testing-can-be-used-to-show-the-presence-of`):

> *Program testing can be used to show the presence of bugs, but never to show their absence!*

So, do not let failures stop you. Learn from them, recognize the mistakes, and try to fix them properly.

How Much Functional Code Do I Need?

A doctor cures a disease using different medicines. The doctor can also vary the dose for different patients. You, as a developer, can use different programming languages to make an application. Based on the requirement criteria, you may also decide how much functional code (or imperative code) you want to use. This is why in Chapter 1 I told you that you can choose the approach (or mix the approaches) that suits your needs best.

Applications of FP

C# gains in popularity every day. It is being used in many domains such as web development, game development, cloud applications, and Android development. At the same time, functional programming is not limited to academia; it is becoming popular in the software industry. You have probably noticed that functional languages like Haskell and F# are growing fast too.

You now know the fundamentals of functional programming. You also know C#. Since C# supports functional programming, you can showcase your skill in all the domains where C# is being used. In fact, by combining the two concepts, you can make powerful applications. Particularly, in a multithreaded environment, by providing support for parallelism, you can take your coding ability to the next level.

The Road Ahead

Congratulations! You have reached the end of the book. Anyone can start a journey, but only a few will complete it with care. You are among the minority who possess the extraordinary capability to cover the distance successfully. I hope that you have enjoyed your learning experience. Return to the discussions, examples, implementations, and Q&A sessions in the book to get even clarity about the topics.

If you are wondering where to go next, let me tell you about my journey in functional programming with C#.

I started using C# in 2005–2006, and I was using it on a regular basis when I joined HP in 2009. Most of the time I worked with Java and C#. You can easily assume that my key focus was on OOP, not on FP. So, when I decided to write this book, I needed to learn many things. Why? Being an OOP lover, I was following a specific thought pattern, and I was trying to solve every problem in an imperative way. But the "functional way of thinking" is quite different. Changing your thinking pattern is much tougher than learning new syntax or rules. This is why I suggest you not hurry. If you come from an OOP background, you need to be patient about functional programming. Remember that true learning comes from continuous practice.

Once I become familiar with FP, I started reading more books and articles on this topic. At the same time, I enrolled myself in different online courses to ensure that I did not miss essential topics. I put forward my best effort to simply these materials to make your learning experience easier as well as enjoyable. This is why once you complete this book, I suggest you go through the materials that I mention in the appendix. Those books, courses, and articles were helpful to me, and I expect that they will be equally effective for you.

Finally, you already know that although C# supports some FP, it is primarily an OOP language. Most code written in C# relies on OOP, not FP. F# is the opposite; it is primarily an FP language with OOP skills. It was designed for FP from the beginning, so it is a lot more natural to use techniques such as currying, immutability by default, pattern matching, HOFs, discriminated unions, and more. The culture around it is FP, so using it will help you develop the "functional way of thinking." F# is also a powerful language and easy to learn, with the professional support of Microsoft. Since both C# and F# are .NET languages, they are interoperable. It is useful when C# developers aim to code in an FP paradigm in an environment with which they are comfortable.

Thank you for choosing this book. Happy coding!

Exercises

E9.1 Can you predict the output of the following code?

```
using LanguageExt;
using static System.Console;

var option = Option<int>.Some(15);
var result = option
    .Bind<int>(x => x * 3)
    .Bind<int>(y => y + 10);
WriteLine(result);
```

E9.2 Can you predict the output of the following code?

```
using LanguageExt;
using static System.Console;

var option = Option<int>.Some(15);

var result2 = option
    .Bind<int>(x => x + 3)
    .Bind<int, int>(y => x * y);
WriteLine(result2);
```

E9.3 Can you predict the output of the following code?

```
using LanguageExt;
using static System.Console;

var option = Option<int>.Some(15);

Func<int, Option<int>> add3 = x => x + 3;
Func<int, int, Option<int>> multiply = (x, y) => x * y;

var result3 = option
    .Bind(x => add3(x)
        .Bind(y => multiply(x, y)));
WriteLine(result3);
```

E9.4 Can you predict the output of the following code?

```
using LanguageExt;
using static System.Console;

Either<Exception, string> either1 = "10";
Func<string, Either<Exception, int>> add4 =
  x => int.Parse(x) + 4;
var result4 = either1.Bind(x => add4(x));
WriteLine(result4);
```

E9.5 Can you predict the output of the following code?

```
using LanguageExt;
using static System.Console;
```

```
Func<double, Either<string, double>> add5 = x => x + 5;
Func<double, double, Either<string, double>> divide =
 (x, y) => y/x +" Done";
var either2 = Either<string, double>.Right(10);
var result5 = either2
    .Bind(x => add5(x)
    , .Bind(y => divide(x, y)));
WriteLine(result5);
```

E9.6 Can you predict the output of the following code?

```
using LanguageExt;
using static System.Console;
Func<int, Either<string, int>> add6 = x => x + 6;
Func<int, int, Either<string, int>> multiplyNumbers =
 (x, y) => x * y;
var either3 = Either<string, int>.Right(10);
var result6 = either3
    .Bind(x => add6(x)
    .Bind(y => multiplyNumbers(x, y)));
WriteLine(result6);
```

E9.7 I have used LanguageExt's Option<T> in this chapter. I have also told you that it is a monad. Can you verify the statement using the following functions?

```
Func<int, Option<int>> f = x => x * 2;
Func<int, Option<double>> g = x => x + 5.5;
```

Summary

This is the last chapter of this book. In brief, it answered the following questions:

- What are some essential C# features for FP?

- How are the Bind and Return functions defined for Option<T> in LanguageExt?

- What is a monad? What are the monad laws?

- How can you use your FP knowledge in the future?

- How can you learn more about FP?

Solutions to Exercises

Here are the solutions for the exercises in this chapter.

E9.1

This program produces the following output:

Some(55)

[Clue: (15*3)+10=55]

E9.2

This program cannot compile. You'll see the following error:

CS0103   The name 'x' does not exist in the current context

E9.3

This program produces the following output:

Some(270)

[Clue: 15*(15+3)=270]

POINT TO NOTE

You have learned that if you replace the following lines:

```
Func<int, Option<int>> add3 = x => x + 3;
Func<int, int, Option<int>> multiply = (x, y) => x * y;
```

with the following lines (using local functions):

```
Option<int> add3(int x) => x + 3;
Option<int> multiply(int x, int y) => x * y;
```

you'll get the same output. The same comment applies to similar codes in this exercise.

E9.4

This program produces the following output:

```
Right(14)
```

[Clue: 10+4=14]

E9.5

This program produces the following output. Notice that the final result is a `string`, not a `double`. This is why the final outcome is in the left state.

```
Left(1.5 Done)
```

[Clue: 10+5=15, 15/10=1.5, 1.5+"Done"=1.5 Done]

E9.6

This program produces the following output. Notice that everything went well and the final result is an `int`, not a `string`. This is why both are in the right state.

```
Right(160)
```

[Clue: 10+6=16, 10*16=160]

E9.7

You have seen that `Option<T>` has both the `Return` function and the `Bind` function. So, `Option<T>` is a monad. The following program shows that it follows the monad laws as well (read the comments for reference). So, it is a proper monad.

```
using LanguageExt;
using static System.Console;

Func<int, Option<int>> f = x => x * 2;
Func<int, Option<double>> g = x => x + 5.5;
var option = Option<int>.Some(15);

// Testing Left Identity:  Return(x).Bind(f) == f(x)

var result1 = option.Bind(f);
WriteLine(result1);
var result2 = f(15);
WriteLine(result2);

// Testing Right Identity:  m.Bind(Return)= m
var result3 = option.Bind(Option<int>.Some);
WriteLine(result3);
var result4 = option;
WriteLine(result4);

// Testing associativity: m.Bind(f).Bind(g)=m.Bind(x=>f(x).Bind(g))
var result5 = option.Bind(f).Bind(g);
WriteLine(result5);
var result6 = option.Bind(x=>f(x).Bind(g));
WriteLine(result6);
```

This program produces the following output:

```
Some(30)
Some(30)
Some(15)
Some(15)
Some(35.5)
Some(35.5)
```

The first two lines in the output confirm the left identity, the next two lines confirm the right identity, and the final two lines confirm the associativity.

Recommended Resources

This appendix lists some useful resources including paid courses that I have gotten many insights from. You can use these resources to learn more about functional programming and other topics.

Books

In the following list, not all the books are exclusively dedicated to C#. Still, I recommend you learn from them because each of them focuses on functional programming (FP). In fact, the last one is my technical reviewer's favorite.

- *Functional Programming in C#* by Enrico Buonanno (Manning Publications Co., 2017)

- *Real-World Functional Programming* by Tomas Petricek with Jon Skeet (Manning Publications Co., 2010)

- *Functional Programming for Dummies* by John Paul Mueller (John Wiley & Sons, 2010)

- *Learn You a Haskell for Great Good!* by Miran Lipovaca (No Starch Press, 2011); also available online at `http://learnyouahaskell.com/`

Documentation

The following list includes some useful documentation. These resources will help you to understand the content of this book.

C#: `https://learn.microsoft.com/en-us/dotnet/csharp/`
NuGet: `https://learn.microsoft.com/en-us/nuget/`
Curryfy: `https://github.com/leandromoh/Curryfy`

© Vaskaran Sarcar 2023
V. Sarcar, *Introducing Functional Programming Using C#*, https://doi.org/10.1007/978-1-4842-9697-4

language-ext: `https://languageext.readthedocs.io/en/latest/README.html`

In addition, you can look at MoreLINQ. Though I have not used this library, many C# developers use it to get helpful extensions for LINQ. You can find more information about it at `https://morelinq.github.io/`.

Courses

The following list includes helpful online courses. At the time of this writing, all the courses charge a fee, but occasionally they offer promotional discounts.

- `https://www.udemy.com/course/functional-programming-deep-dive-with-c-sharp/?kw=functional+C%23&src=sac`

- `https://www.linkedin.com/learning/advanced-c-sharp-functional-programming-patterns/functional-programming-pat terns?autoplay=true&u=93557497`

- `https://www.udemy.com/course/functional-csharp/`

Other Resources

You have seen various online resources in the discussions and the "Q&A Session" sections throughout this book. If interested, you can take a detailed look at those resources to learn more about those specific topics.

Index

© Vaskaran Sarcar 2023
V. Sarcar, *Introducing Functional Programming Using C#*, https://doi.org/10.1007/978-1-4842-9697-4